Nonfoundationalism

—historical inquiry cannot be the basis for the faith in christ; yet it cannot dissolve this faith by the questions it asks, because it cannot authoritatively preclude the historicity of the life, death & resurr. of Jesus

—the resurrection of Jesus is the reason for Xn theology

in a sense, doing theology from the gospel is a kind of foundationalism — yet it another sense it is not

—conversation & dialogue with other worldviews is essential, otherwise the gospel is incomprehensible, unintelligable

for book proposal:
—approach I use is critical engagement with modern scientific worldviews, from perspective of the gospel

GUIDES TO
THEOLOGICAL
INQUIRY

Edited by Kathryn Tanner of Yale University and Paul
Lakeland of Fairfield University, *Guides to Theological
Inquiry* are intended to introduce theologians, scholars,
students, and clergy to those academic methods, disciplines, and movements that are most germane to contemporary theology. Neither simple surveys nor exhaustive monographs, these short books will provide solid,
reliable, programmatic statements of the main lines or
workings of their topics and assessments of their theological impact.

Forthcoming titles in the series include *Hermeneutics* by
Francis Schüssler Fiorenza, *Feminist Theory* by Serene
Jones, *Literary Criticism* by David Dawson, *Critical Social
Theory* by Gary M. Simpson, *Theories of Culture* by Kath-
ryn Tanner, and *Postmodernity* by Paul Lakeland.

GUIDES TO
THEOLOGICAL
INQUIRY

Nonfoundationalism

☙

John E. Thiel

Fortress Press/Minneapolis

Rev. Anders S. June

Also by John E. Thiel
Imagination and Authority:
Theological Authorship in the
Modern Tradition
(Fortress Press, 1991)

NONFOUNDATIONALISM
Guides to Theological Inquiry series

Cover design: Terry Bentley
Author photo: Kevin Wolfthal

Library of Congress Cataloging-in-Publication Data

Thiel, John E.
    Nonfoundationalism / John E. Thiel.
       p.   cm.
    Includes bibliographical references and index.
    ISBN 0-8006-2692-3 :
    1. Philosophical theology.   2. Knowledge, Theory of (Religion)
I. Title.
BT40.T44   1994
230'.01—dc20   94-2159
                                               CIP

Manufactured in the U.S.A.   AF 1–2692

98   97   96   95   94   1   2   3   4   5   6   7   8   9   10

In memory of
Lucille Palumbo Cook
and
Richard Victor Cook

Contents

Foreword

No self-sufficient enterprise, Christian theology always proceeds in intellectual dialogue with other forms of inquiry. Perhaps it was a habit fostered by chance in the Hellenistic milieu, in which Christianity achieved its greatest initial success. Perhaps it was a necessary outcome of its desire to speak from a Christian point of view about the whole of life. Whatever the reason, theology had philosophy as its dialogue partner from the first and for much of its history. With the contraction, however, of philosophy's scope in the late nineteenth century and the parceling out of its domain to the disciplines of the modern academy (economics, politics, psychology, etc.), the theologian's task of keeping up this dialogue became more difficult. Guides to Theological Inquiry aims to ease this burden by familiarizing people with major new academic movements, disciplines, and trends and clarifying ways in which they might be of continuing importance for theological investigation.

One such movement on the contemporary academic scene to which growing numbers of theologians feel attracted is nonfoundationalism. Now spanning many different academic fields, it functions in almost the role of a litmus test of intellectual respectability. Nonfoundationalism has many of its roots in philosophical arguments of an often technical nature. John Thiel's reliable guidance through this material and the broader conclusions to be drawn from it will be of particular aid to readers without a great deal of philosophical background. Even the most informed readers, the so-far wary and the eager advocates of nonfoundationalism alike, will be edified by Thiel's fresh perspective and measured judgments concerning the benefits and dangers of nonfoundationalism for theology.

KATHRYN TANNER

Preface

One might expect a book published in a series of "Guides to Theological Inquiry" to sketch the various uses of a theological method or to explore disciplines useful in contemporary theology. Many of the books published in this series will have that aim as, in many respects, does this one. Yet I think the reader would do better to see this volume as an examination of interpretive sensibilities that attend methods, rather than as a study of any particular one. It introduces philosophical arguments against "foundations" for knowledge and the implications of these arguments for theological interpretation. Nonfoundationalism is a rubric that can cover a wide field of critical play. In the following pages, the term refers to contemporary philosophical approaches to the logical and disciplinary criticism of knowledge. I have not sought to extend the application of the term to deconstructive readings of texts, though nonfoundationalism could be understood in that way.

The issues, works, and thinkers examined in these pages are illustrative, and prescribed limitations on its length prevent this book from being an exhaustive study. The reader dealing with the issues of nonfoundational criticism for the first time will quickly notice a consonance between this editorial limitation and the subject matter. Chapter 1 introduces the reader to the work of nonfoundational philosophers by addressing several themes that have been prominent in their work. Chapter 2 examines the work of theologians who, implicitly and explicitly, have highlighted the value of the nonfoundational perspective for theological interpretation. Chapter 3 explores the critical issues at stake in how this perspective has been and may continue to be put to the service of theological interpretation. I am grateful above all to Kathryn E. Tanner, Yale University, who edited this work. Her careful, critical reading of its drafts improved the manuscript at every step of the way. Paul F. Lakeland and Thomas J. Regan, S.J., Fairfield University, made many helpful suggestions that enhanced the clarity of argumentation and style. Paul Lakeland has done me this favor so many times that an acknowledgment here is but the latest event in a history of gratitude. Roger F. Gibson, Jr., Washington University, criticized an early version of the first chapter and saved me from error on a couple of points in the presentation of Willard Van Orman Quine's thought. His generous willingness to read my manuscript reminded me how much scholarly activity can depend on the kindness of strangers. Michael West and David Lott of Fortress Press ably guided these pages to print. Dorothea Cook Thiel has always given me encouragement and support in my work that stand unseen on every page. This book is dedicated to the memory of her parents, a continuing source of inspiration to our family.

JOHN E. THIEL

1

Nonfoundationalism as Philosophical Criticism

Twentieth-century thought increasingly has had to reckon with the judgments and claims of an approach to philosophical criticism called nonfoundationalism. No particular philosopher can be named as the founder of this critical approach, nor does a school of thinkers faithful to the tenets of nonfoundationalism exist. At most, one can speak of a commitment to a style of philosophizing shared by a number of thinkers, and often in very different ways. Whether this commitment advances the concerns of American pragmatism, sets the direction of the "linguistic turn," or fuels the suspicion of theory in a host of contemporary philosophies, it is always critical of the epistemological assumption that there are "foundations" for knowledge, noninferential principles whose certainty and stability ground other epistemic claims. To use the imagery suggested by Ernest Sosa, nonfoundationalists consider it far more appropriate to understand knowledge as a "raft" rather than as a "pyramid," as relative claims, at best coherent, floating on the ever-moving currents of time and culture rather than as certain truths timelessly fixed in never-shifting sands.[1]

Any discussion of nonfoundationalism as philosophical criticism, or as philosophical criticism put to the service of theological interpretation, must begin by noting the negative terms in which its critical perspective is cast, and the problems that this negative designation creates for situating the claims of nonfoundationalism. The varieties of nonfoundationalism may eventually take shape in detailed expositions that justifiably can be described as philosophical positions or stances. Broadly considered, however, at the level of its intellectual impetus, nonfoundationalism is not a position or stance in its own right but a judgment about what is *not* philosophically tenable. Nonfoundationalism is gainsaying. It is a form of criticism that assesses the logical viability of the most traditional assumptions about knowing and finds them wanting.

This negative way of characterizing its stance makes any effort to clarify nonfoundationalism a second-order activity, a matter of delineating the foundationalism that nonfoundationalism rejects. And even here the problem of negative definition continues. The term *foundationalism* suggests an intellectual claim in its own right, a substantive position that seemingly would admit of definition much easier than a view that names itself contrapuntally. Foundationalism, however, is nearly always a pejorative label that nonfoundationalists give to philosophical positions found guilty in their court of criticism. Foundationalism could be defined from a logical perspective as the view that mediately justified beliefs require epistemic support for their validity in immediately justified beliefs, or from a disciplinary perspective as the view that systems of knowledge, in content and method, require first principles. These definitions, though, typically are the property of the nonfoundationalist and are offered as expressions of foundationalism's inherent deficiencies.

To the degree that both foundationalism and nonfoundationalism are mutually constituted positions that appear in a wide range of nuanced views, they elude the abstraction of formal definition. Consequently, our understanding of the issues at stake in the philosophical critique of foundationalism cannot depend on the guidance of precise taxonomies. Instead, in the pages to follow, our approach will be descriptive. By considering representative arguments by several nonfoundational philosophers, we will be able to appreciate their concerns about what knowledge is and what it is not, as well as the variety of ways in which nonfoundationalists explain their views and the views of their opponents.

This chapter will explore nonfoundationalism as philosophical criticism in several steps. It begins by sketching the claims to "foundations" for knowledge in the modern epistemological tradition, exemplified here by the work of Descartes, the British empiricists, and the German idealists, and goes on to consider the emergence of the nonfoundational perspective in the criticism of this tradition offered by Charles Sanders Peirce, William James, John Dewey, and Ludwig Wittgenstein. The lion's share of the chapter will examine the specific arguments against "foundations" for knowledge advanced by Wilfrid Sellars, Willard Van Orman Quine, Richard Rorty, Richard Bernstein, Donald Davidson, and Michael Williams. Although the work of these philosophers is the primary focus of this chapter, we should keep in mind that our interest will settle later in the book on the value of their critical insights for theology.

Modern Epistemology, Pragmatism, and the Linguistic Turn

While contemporary philosophers have contributed most to the explicit development of nonfoundational criticism, their views had precedence in the work of earlier generations of American and European philosophers who challenged the assumptions of modern epistemology. Contemporary nonfoundational philosophy can only be appreciated in light of this intellectual history, which the limitations of a slim volume require us to sketch in broad strokes. As we consider the main philosophical currents against which nonfoundationalism took its stance and from which it was shaped, we would do well to think of this modern history as a narrative of epistemic authority. René Descartes is a central character in this story not only because of his influence on modern understandings of the philosophical project but also because his thought has come to be represented as a paradigm of foundationalism by many nonfoundational critics.

Ever since G. W. F. Hegel's lectures on the history of philosophy, it has been customary to date the beginning of modern philosophy from the work of René Descartes (1596–1650). Hegel marked Descartes's efforts to construct a "metaphysics of the understanding" as a significant shift in the history of philosophy, one that he believed anticipated and culminated in his own philosophy of absolute knowledge.[2] His assessment of Descartes's work as a watershed in the history of philosophy has proved true, even if not for Hegel's rather self-centered estimation of its importance. Although many would argue that Descartes's modern preoccupation with a "metaphysics of the understanding" has been eclipsed by postmodern approaches to the philosophical task in which "metaphysics" and even "understanding" are questionable categories, the epistemological concerns he made central to intellectual inquiry remain on the disciplinary agenda of philosophy, be it modern or postmodern.

Descartes's influential role in configuring the rubric of "modern" philosophy derives from the content of his thought, but more particularly from his methodological expectation that philosophy has a need to ground its project, to establish first principles or foundations on which the edifice of knowledge may be built. Premodern Western philosophy, by virtue of its commitment to the intellectual heritage of Platonism, tended to assume rather than to establish the foundations for philosophical inquiry and speculation, locating these in some form of metaphysical reality—whether the Platonic idea, the Aristotelian form, or the divine existence itself. Descartes continues this epistemological tradition by claiming in the fourth of his *Meditations on First Philosophy* (1641) that true knowledge is discovered in the mind's assent to clear and distinct ideas that in turn derive their epistemic authority from their ultimate origin in God.[3] Descartes, however, parts company with the premodern Platonic tradition in his judgment that the first principles of philosophy cannot be presented in the course of speculative inquiry. For Descartes, the philosopher's *first* task is to establish the principles on which knowledge rests since, in his judgment, even the possibility of rational certainty depends on the authority of such epistemic foundations.

In his *Discourse on Method* (1637), Descartes uncovers the foundations of knowledge by appealing to the mind's most reflexive experience of certainty. Wary of mistaking the customary for the certain in the search for philosophy's first principles, Descartes puts all his beliefs and assumptions on trial before the court of radical doubt. The only assertion he finds capable of an unassailable defense in the face of skeptical prosecution is the self-assurance that consciousness is indeed on trial, that the thinking subject indubitably is doubting. Reason, Descartes insists, "tells us clearly that all our ideas or notions must have some foundation of truth,"⁴ and that the certainty of doubting establishes such a foundation within the doubter's own act of reflection:

> I noticed that whilst I thus wished to think all things false, it was absolutely essential that the "I" who thought this should be somewhat, and remarking that this truth "*I think, therefore I am*" was so certain and so assured that all the most extravagant suppositions brought forward by the sceptics were incapable of shaking it, I came to the conclusion that I could receive it without scruple as the first principle of the Philosophy for which I was seeking.⁵

This statement stands in Descartes's philosophy not as a conclusion, but as a starting point that establishes the possibility of knowledge. By imbuing the *cogito* with the authority of a philosophical first principle, Descartes understood its certainty to be reflected in the order of rational inquiry in general and, indirectly at least, in every particular act of knowing.

Whether philosophical inquiry in the generations after Descartes continued the project of modern philosophy by following the path of empiricism or rationalism, it nonetheless accepted his assumption that philosophical reflection must determine its foundation or ground—at least by affirmation, preferably by demonstration—before it can proceed with the business of speculation or criticism. Empiricists in the British tradition, like John Locke (1632–1704) and David Hume (1711–1776), argued that sense experience and not ideas provides a grounding for philosophical inquiry. While the empiricists in no way compromised the power accorded to the act of understanding by Descartes, they attributed the constitution, and thus the authority, of sensible ideas to the sense data from which they believed them to be formed. The immediacy of sense experience provided the empiricists with a foundation for philosophy that they judged to be clearer and more distinct than the mind's self-reflective ideas.

Idealists in the German tradition, like Immanuel Kant (1724–1804), Johann G. Fichte (1762–1814), Friedrich W. J. Schelling (1775–1854), and Georg W. F. Hegel (1770–1831), argued against the empiricists by claiming that the givenness of the mind's ideas, their a priori character, posed principles for a first philosophy. Kant defined the project of moral philosophy as laying the foundations for a practical metaphysics, a philosophy that would "seek out and establish *the supreme principle of morality*."[6] Fichte sought the "primordial, absolutely unconditioned first principle of all human knowledge" in the experience of self-identity, for him the essence of human consciousness itself.[7] Schelling claimed that the foundations for human intellection lay in the mind's access to the divine ideas, as these could be fathomed in their historical development.[8] Hegel insisted that the ground of the system of knowledge that philosophy aspired to be was an elevated consciousness of the historical movement of *Geist*, "Truth, aware of what it is."[9] The idealists, then, all sought a grounding for philosophy in the structure of understanding or in the higher reaches of reasoning, and, having established such first principles, invoked their authority to justify their speculative endeavors.

While the empiricists sought foundations for knowledge in the givenness of sense experience to the mind and the idealists in the mind's innate ability to transcend the sensible, both groups of philosophical practitioners continued to promulgate the most basic assumptions of the Cartesian project. Both empiricists and idealists assumed that philosophy is largely an exercise in epistemology. Both assumed that epistemological explanation involves naming the foundations of knowing as a requisite, first step in the philosophical task. Both assumed that the foundations of knowing, however chthonic or ethereal, are located in the human mind, thus establishing the mind's authority for evaluating or even constituting the noetic world. With regard to these shared assumptions, the empiricists and idealists comprise a single epistemological tradition which, in one way or another, remains committed to the orientations of philosophical method and inquiry proposed by Descartes.

Precursors

The nonfoundationalists we will examine in more detail regard this epistemological tradition as foundationalist, a pejorative judgment expressing their view that Cartesian epistemology justifies claims to knowledge, and even the discipline of philosophy itself, by illegitimate appeal to the authority of universal principles of understanding. Contemporary philosophers like Quine, Rorty, and Bernstein, however, were not the first philosophers in the modern tradition to register this objection. Their precursors were the pragmatists and philosophers of language of the late nineteenth and early twentieth centuries. Our narrative of the birth of the nonfoundational perspective in modern philosophy can advance by considering their redefinition of the philosophical task as a search for contextual rather than universal truth.

William James (1842–1910) is the philosopher whose thought is most readily associated with the doctrine of pragmatism, but it is Charles Sanders Peirce (1839–1914) who more deservedly is remembered as the originator of this philosophical approach. According to Peirce, pragmatism is "not a theory" devised in special circumstances but an analytical procedure committed to the view that "the meaning of an intellectual conception [is configured by] what practical consequences might conceivably result by necessity from the truth of that conception." These practical consequences exhaust any conception's intelligibility, for "the sum of these consequences will constitute the entire meaning of the conception."[10] Peirce recognized that this maxim could be helpful as a principle for the conduct of life in general, but as a systematic philosopher he was much more interested in its value for intellectual inquiry, as an investigative rule for every branch of science.[11]

In his 1868 essay, "Some Consequences of Four Incapacities," Peirce anticipated the development of his doctrine of pragmatism by expressing his dissatisfaction with the most basic assumptions of Cartesian philosophy. The "spirit of Cartesianism" attempted to advance beyond scholasticism's essentially religious commitment to the mysteries of faith by claiming that the "ultimate test of certainty is to be found in the individual consciousness" that has successfully run the gauntlet of radical doubt and reached the assurance of its own first principles.[12] The expected consequences of such certainty, however, prove wanting in actual practice. Philosophers of reputation disagree, even vehemently, about the definition of first principles, to say nothing of the inferences that might be drawn from them. The fact of philosophical disagreement about what should produce unquestioning assent shows the folly of Descartes's confidence in the purifying powers of doubt. For Peirce, Cartesian doubt is "mere self-deception, and not real doubt" since it too quickly asserts the certainty of first principles where none exists.[13] Philosophical inquiry cannot be based on the supposed verities of individual consciousness but can only be conducted amid the prejudices, agreements, disagreements, and, at best, consensus of those committed to the pursuit of truth. It is, in other words, a continuing search "for the *community* of philosophers."[14] Appealing to a now famous image, Peirce proposed that "reasoning should not form a chain which is no stronger than its weakest link, but a cable whose fibers may be ever so slender, provided they are sufficiently numerous and intimately connected."[15]

Pragmatism, or pragmaticism as Peirce later described his doctrine, is a procedure for the clarification of thinking. It refuses, though, to follow the Cartesian lead in making a particular aspect of thinking the final warrant of any and all acts of knowing. Peirce claimed that the cognitive faculties do not produce certain epistemic principles. The cognition that is their issue is a groundless network of relations in which "every cognition is determined logically by previous cognitions."[16] Thinking does not offer a foundation on which a complex of higher truths might be built, but is a restless activity ever vexed by doubt as it searches for the relative quiescence of belief. The production of belief, Peirce holds, "is the sole function of thought."[17]

By "belief" Peirce does not refer to an explicitly religious experience. In fact, Peirce usually cites religious experience or doctrine in his writings as illustrations of the absurd. Belief is a subjective disposition that satisfies the yearnings of thought. It can only be reached through careful inquiry in which the quibbles of doubt are heard and answered. Belief, however, is not an intellectual abstraction deemed more worthy of commitment than others. However subtly philosophers may differentiate between their most valued ideas, there is for Peirce "no distinction of meaning so fine as to consist in anything but a possible difference of practice."[18] Belief relieves the irritation of doubt by establishing a "rule of action" or "habit" for the individual's practical conduct in the world.[19]

Beliefs supply a considered framework for the concrete decisions, commitments, and actions of the individual. Beliefs, however, are neither self-certain nor exclusively the property of individual consciousness. They are only relatively secure in the guidance they offer to practice and are themselves subject to revision as they encounter differing beliefs in the community of inquiry. For Peirce, pragmatism is a doctrine that recognizes the authority of the community of inquiry since practice, the pragmatic measure of truth, necessarily occurs in a social, and not a mental, setting. And in this social setting, what we commonly call "truth" flourishes in a context of meaning reached, perpetuated, and revised within the community of inquiry itself. Although he was an epistemological realist who maintained the existence of reality and its truth apart from the thinking subject, Peirce was uncomfortable with the traditional ways of explaining the subject's apprehension of truth as a correspondence of the self to the world or the world to the self. For Peirce, truth is ascertained neither through the empiricist's alignment of the mind to the object nor through the rationalist's conformity of the object to the mind. Truth issues from the network of beliefs shared by the community of inquiry, beliefs that have shown themselves to be respectable rules for practice by virtue of their capacity to yield meaningful results.

Pierce's lead in explaining truth as a coherent system of meaningful beliefs validated by practice was followed by fellow pragmatists such as William James and John Dewey (1859–1952). For James, truth is not a quality inherent in the nature of things but a process through which an idea is verified by events. True ideas are those "we can assimilate, validate, corroborate and verify," whereas false ideas are those not susceptible to these procedures. The only difference between truth and falsity lies in "the practical difference it makes to us to have true ideas."[20] In a rather flamboyant turn of phrase, James described the power of the true idea as its "cash-value," its capacity to fund the meaningfulness of its practical effects.[21] John Dewey was less concerned than Peirce and James with sketching a pragmatic method for philosophical inquiry. Philosophical inquiry, he maintains, is an ad hoc procedure that "starts from an effort to get out of some trouble, actual or menacing."[22] Experience does not reveal certainties on which such an inquiry can be based, but provides instead evidence by which our ideas and judgments may be continually verified. The meaningfulness of experience waxes or wanes in proportion to its practical effects. For Dewey, "things gain meaning when they are used as *means to bring about consequences* . . . , or as standing for *consequences* for which we have to discover *means*."[23]

A detailed study of the philosophies of Peirce, James, and Dewey would take note of the many ways in which their views differ. For our purposes it is important to consider how their common concerns represent the beginnings of nonfoundational sensibilities in the modern philosophical tradition. First, the pragmatists all rejected the Cartesian method of establishing the first principles of philosophy as a necessary propaedeutic to philosophical inquiry itself. Second, all rejected the metaphysics of understanding in which either sense experience or ideas were privileged as the authoritative basis of knowing, as the foundations for the truth of a philosophical system. Third, all rejected the traditional rationalist or empiricist definition of truth as an isolated correspondence between self and world, affirming instead an understanding of truth as a social context of meaning shaped by the practical implications of ideas. This contextual and foundationless conception of truth was the most characteristic mark of the philosophies of pragmatism. But it also came to distinguish many forms of twentieth-century philosophy which criticized modern epistemology by appealing to language as a vehicle of meaning. The work of Ludwig Wittgenstein (1889–1951) may serve as an example of this approach, often described as the "linguistic turn" in the modern philosophical tradition.

Language and Meaning

In his *Philosophical Investigations*, a late work published posthumously in 1953, Wittgenstein argues that meaning of any sort behaves like a language. A language has many structural features, but the most intriguing and philosophically instructive for Wittgenstein is the grammar by which it abides. While language as elementary expression may be a universally human phenomenon, the grammars of this language or that are formed in the most culture-specific and practical circumstances of social life. Wittgenstein finds this contingent and particular quality of linguistic meaning to be helpful in understanding the workings of the intellect and the will. Just as the meaningfulness of a language is governed by its grammar, so too are the activities of thinking, deciding, and acting defined by the particular frame of reference in which their meaningful practice thrives. Wittgenstein, in fact, considered this linguistic analogy to be so apt that he referred to meaningful practices in general as "language-games." Language-games, like games in general, are not universally purposive but defined by the specific rules which govern their play. Like grammatical constructs, the rules of a language-game are "arbitrary." They are products of the coherent system they regulate rather than the starting points for the play of meaning that engenders them.[24]

Applying these views to the process of thinking, Wittgenstein concludes that the rules of logic are not principles inherent in the nature of thought, any more than grammatical structures are inherent in the nature of language. The logical principles that reason follows are every bit the product of culture, of trial and error, and of practical application as are the rules of other meaning systems. Logical order is determined by the circumstances of its use, circumstances which are thoroughly social and fixed by convention. Wittgenstein insists that there can be no private language that defies the practical and public setting of meaning as use, and so no way in which the inner realm of subjectivity or any of its issue can be privileged as the basis of knowing. "What I hold fast to," he insists, "is not *one* proposition but a nest of propositions."[25] There are no first principles on which a context of meaning rests but only the context itself, a network of interrelated and mutually constitutive meanings.

Wittgenstein maintains that the philosopher "cannot give [language] any foundation. . . ." Philosophy "simply puts everything before us, and neither explains nor deduces anything."[26] The utterly contextual character of language-games precludes the possibility of fashioning some final purpose or meaning from the ways in which they work. The philosophical task involves the description of a language-game's fabric of meaning, not speculation about which of its threads holds all the others in place. At least indirectly, then, Wittgenstein judges the proper role of philosophy to be the criticism of traditional conceptions of it as a discipline. Philosophical investigations of how thinking "means" must also expose the pretensions of universal perspectives, truth claims, and methods that so easily pass for legitimate philosophizing. Like the pragmatists, Wittgenstein considers metaphysical or dogmatic understandings of truth to be exaggerations of the actual and more modest situations in which human beings make and appreciate meaning. He is satisfied to speak of truth as a value shaped by the vast complex of ad hoc circumstances that life offers and which life itself is.

We have seen that this view of meaning as a network of practically verified beliefs was held in common by the forerunners of contemporary nonfoundational philosophers. Peirce, James, Dewey, and Wittgenstein sought to avoid Cartesianism's most capricious assumptions by arguing for the cogency of a contextual understanding of truth that did not expect claims to be justified by a privileged noetic certainty. The nonfoundational philosophies of Sellars, Quine, Rorty, and Davidson, to which we now turn, developed this insight in ways that the pragmatists could not have anticipated. But these more recent contributions to nonfoundational criticism made the pragmatists' conception of truth, and the renunciation of traditional epistemology for which it calls, central to their intellectual vision. Indeed, the paradigm of practical contextuality has presented such a formidable challenge to the Cartesian heritage that Descartes's epistemological approach is now largely regarded as a fallacy by contemporary philosophers. Nonfoundationalists, however, are rarely dismissive of this fallacy's seductive power and of its ability to present itself in numerous guises, all of which promise an epistemic security, completeness, and stability that knowledge does not possess. In the pages to follow we will explore the various ways in which nonfoundationalists identify and argue against the foundationalist fallacy.

Mental Myths: Sellars and Quine on the Limitations of Theory

While the nonfoundational positions examined in this chapter criticize the Cartesian tradition, it is important to realize that the epistemological assumptions of Cartesianism are not restricted to the domain of philosophy. Wilfrid Sellars and Willard Van Orman Quine are two philosophers who have worked to expose the baselessness of Cartesian assumptions in the theorizing that all disciplines offer to explain their subject matter. Sellars and Quine do not agree completely in their criticism of Cartesian theoretical assumptions. Both, however, address the high degree to which disciplinary methods embrace a view of the mind at work that is little more than a fantasy. Our discussion of Sellars and Quine will focus on their shared understanding of epistemic foundations as mental myths, and on the power of such myths in universal explanations or theories.

The Myth of the Given

Wilfrid Sellars sees the aim of philosophy as "the reflective knowing one's way around in the scheme of things."[27] Philosophy traditionally has been preoccupied with the business of "knowing that," with the mind's discovery and possession of truth, but Sellars thinks a more adequate concern of philosophy is the business of "knowing how," of investigating the workings of the conceptual schemes we call disciplines and evaluating their logical coherence. In this respect, philosophy cannot simply be counted as one of the many specialty disciplines. It has the responsibility of proving the integrity of the disciplines by assessing the assumptions and theories they embrace as justifications for their claims to knowledge. In this role of overseer, philosophy must expose the axioms that disciplines hold dear but that cannot pass the test of close, critical scrutiny. One of the most influential of these axioms, one which appears as a primal fallacy amid the basic assumptions of a host of disciplines, is what Sellars calls the "Myth of the Given."

In a well-known essay entitled "Empiricism and the Philosophy of Mind," Sellars explains that the myth of the given is conceived in several ways. Many who attack the notion of givenness understand it to be the "idea that there are inner episodes, whether thoughts or so-called 'immediate experiences,' to which each of us has privileged access."[28] Sellars, however, does not consider the affirmation of inner episodes or privileged access to them to be epistemically problematic as such. The givenness of experience, the fact that it presents itself to subjects in particular modes and within particular circumstances, is part and parcel of the human condition. Givenness becomes problematic when a certain dimension of experience is imbued with authority and regarded as a foundation for the other claims to knowledge in a conceptual scheme. For Sellars a more correct description of the myth of the given is expressed in "the idea that knowledge of [inner] episodes furnishes *premises* on which empirical knowledge rests as on a foundation."[29] While Sellars believes this to be the most widespread form of the myth, he still considers this depiction to be far removed from the myth's most cherished assumptions.

As a philosopher of empiricist inclinations, Sellars takes for granted that rationalist versions of the myth are rather easily seen for the logical fallacies they are. He believes, though, that the tacit assumptions of sense-datum epistemologies are just as susceptible to the myth of the given as idealist accounts of knowing. In fact, the empiricist version of the myth, which Sellars thinks to be its most consequential form, often eludes philosophical detection because the scientific disciplines that draw their conclusions from empirical method are commonly believed to be incapable of naively professing allegiance to unverifiable principles.

Even if there were foundations for knowledge, the lion's share of the knowledge we value would still be inferential in character, that is, knowledge inferred from, or posited as a warranted conclusion based on, other warranted claims respected in the community of reason. Empiricists typically criticize idealist epistemologies for their unjustified appeal to conceptual first principles. Rationalists treat them as noninferential knowledge, as foundations for the edifice of knowledge that are immediately and authoritatively given, and not themselves the product of inference. But, Sellars argues, the empiricists' rush to criticize rationalist epistemologies frequently leads them to overlook their own unwarranted assumption that sense experience itself constitutes a noninferential knowledge, a foundation on which empirical knowledge is based. However tacitly this association between sense experience and noninferential knowledge is made, the result, Sellars points out, is that sensing is equated with "being conscious," and the impressions of sense with the unquestionable "facts" of consciousness. The most basic plot of this empiricist telling of the myth of the given is virtually indistinguishable from its rationalist version, as sense data are imbued with the same authoritative givenness that the empiricist refuses to recognize in the idealist's conceptual first principles.

Sellars argues that an examination of ordinary descriptions of sense experience finds no reason to regard a sense datum as a "*cognitive* or *epistemic* fact."[30] It is the case that sense data often reach expression as assertive statements of fact. But speakers just as often formulate their descriptions of even the most common appearances—colors, for example—with a tentativeness and reserve that expresses not a fact but a "report" about how something "looks" at a particular time and under certain conditions. Logical scrutiny of this "reporting" or "looks" language, however, reveals the unjustifiability of regarding sense data as conveyors of foundational facts. The propositional expression of any sense datum— "This looks green," for example—presupposes the concept of "being green," as well as an immense network of other concepts like "color," "under standard circumstances," "at this time," and so on to the point that all horizons in the speaker's conceptual world are indirectly stated in the sense datum's simple reporting. For Sellars, these concepts are formed in a "long history of acquiring *piecemeal* habits of response to various objects in various circumstances," and come to noetic life in such mutual interdependence that "one has *no* concept pertaining to the observable properties of physical objects . . . unless one has them all. . . ."[31]

The heart of the myth of the given is the idea "that observation . . . is constituted by certain self-authenticating nonverbal episodes, the authority of which is transmitted to verbal and quasiverbal performances when these performances are made 'in conformity with the semantical rules of the language. . . .'" Within the myth, the givenness of these episodes defines their authority as "the unmoved movers of empirical knowledge."[32] The logic of the language of "looks," however, demonstrates that even the knowing that comes from sensing, the alleged noninferential foundation of empirical knowledge, cannot achieve intelligibility apart from reference to the inferential knowledge it supposedly grounds. For Sellars, this reciprocity between more basic and more complex modes of inferential knowledge does not compromise the authority of knowledge itself, but only the foundationalist authority of the myth of the given. "For empirical knowledge," Sellars states, "like its sophisticated extension, science, is rational, not because it has a *foundation* but because it is a self-correcting enterprise which can put *any* claim in jeopardy, though not *all* at once."[33]

This conclusion has implications not only for the framework of grand epistemological assumptions, like the myth of the given, but also for the more discrete explanatory frameworks called "theories." A theory, Sellars argues, is not a universal principle deduced from a body of gathered experience or data. The common understanding of theories as conceptual or empirical derivations of laws is but a diminished version of the myth of the given, reflecting the myth in its assumption that a theory's worth is measured by its ability to articulate a nontheoretical order dwelling in the nature of things or experience. This inflated regard for the explanatory power of theories, then, takes them to be foundationalist accounts for domains of knowledge. But if knowledge does not rest on noninferential principles, then theories cannot be expressions of the coherence that such principles supposedly lend to inferential knowledge.

Although the commonplace understanding of theories proves to be logically deficient, Sellars does not conclude that theories are devoid of meaning. Their meaning, however, exhibits the modesty of a posteriori reasoning. Rightly understood, a theory is an explanatory approximation to a truth that is contextual, defined by the parameters of the evidence it seeks to explain. Theories are "principles of explanation . . . for the inductive generalizations in [the] framework [of observation] . . . which in their turn serve as principles of explanation for particular matters of fact."[34] They describe how a body of knowledge exhibits faithfulness to the evidence it recognizes. In Sellars's words, theories "explain laws by explaining why the objects of the domain in question obey the laws that they do to the extent that they do."[35] If this definition seems circular it is because Sellars sees theories as descriptions of reasonable coherence offered from *within* a rational system, as accounts of the inductive processes by which the system infers its meaning from the groundless dialectic between sensing and conceiving. Like science, which might very well be considered a macrotheory, microtheories offer self-correcting appraisals of how the world of constructed meaning behaves.

Meaning as Use

Willard Van Orman Quine shares Sellars's suspicion of customary views of theoretical explanation. Like Sellars, his suspicion reflects his commitment to the broad concerns of empiricism, though to an empiricism purged of the foundationalism usually latent in this philosophical stance. Roger Gibson has described Quine's position as "enlightened empiricism" to distinguish it from the positivistic empiricism of Rudolf Carnap and his colleagues in the Vienna Circle of the 1920s and 1930s. The Vienna Circle typically sought to deduce the truths of the natural world from sense data and to translate sensible truths into the language of science, itself the measure of understanding. In Quine's judgment, the empiricist project so conceived is yet another expression of the mistaken Cartesian assumption that authentic understanding can only be achieved by defining and applying first principles of knowing. Quine agrees that the empiricist's rather than the rationalist's path is the appropriate one for the philosopher to tread, but he rejects both the destination and the gait of Carnap and his school. The goal of empirical analysis, Quine holds, is not the deduction of truth from sense data. Empirical analysis has the more modest aim of piecing together an ad hoc theory drawn exclusively from sensory evidence.[36]

Quine's understanding of the task of philosophy is shaped by his understanding of the rootedness of knowledge in sense experience. All that we call knowledge is the neurological consequence of activated nerve endings, which Quine describes in strictly behaviorist terms. Quine rejects any rationalist or, for that matter, traditionally empiricist manner of accounting for human knowledge. Epistemology, if it has any value at all, must function as a branch of a psychology oriented toward the natural sciences. Acknowledging his philosophical kinship with Dewey's naturalism, Quine asserts that "knowledge, mind, and meaning are part of the same world that they have to do with, and . . . are to be studied in the same empirical spirit that animates natural science."[37] Science, in turn, is a "conceptual bridge of our own making, linking sensory stimulation to sensory stimulation."[38] For Quine, there is no role for philosophy to play as an "a priori propaedeutic or groundwork for science." It presents "no external vantage point" from which knowledge can be expounded, and so "no first philosophy." Rather, philosophy is "continuous with science."[39] It is a form of empirical investigation that critically and continually describes the process by which sensory evidence is formed into the web of concepts that make up science or knowledge.

Science certainly attends to the right formation of concepts. But that process, for Quine, cannot take place apart from the formation of words, sentences, and the entire system of meaning that language is. Indeed, what we regard as meaningful at the level of intellectual experience—concepts and judgments—can only be deemed so in relation to the use to which meaning is put in language. Quine insists that "meaning is what it does," and what it does is place value on sensory stimulations in particular conditions or circumstances. Meaning is not a transcendental quality in which meaningful sentences share or participate, but a function of behavior. This stance does not entail the judgment that meaning is so localized in specific instances of its use that it cannot be shared, as though it possessed no communal dimensions. Quine affirms the breadth of meaning, but in the same behavioral terms consistently employed in his philosophy. Sentences are semantically equivalent "if their use is the same . . . [or] if their utterance would be prompted by the same stimulatory situations."[40]

The Myth of the Museum

The behavioral understanding of language for which Quine argues could only admit of a functional perspective on meaning. And if meaning is the use to which sentences are put, then it would make no sense to speak of foundations for such meaning. The circumstantial nature of use dashes the expectation for an abiding certainty that foundationalism would make the measure of knowledge. Quine recognizes, of course, that accounts of meaning in theoretical explanations of all sorts frequently adopt foundationalist assumptions, even if unwittingly. One does not have to adopt foundations for knowing as blatant as Descartes's indubitable *cogito*, or Locke's confidence in sense experience, or Kant's a priori categories of the understanding in order to be guilty of foundationalism. The foundationalist error can steal into epistemic claims in the structure of the mental scheme within which such claims are conceived, and in this manner foundationalism becomes an assumption so generalized and diffused in theoretical explanations that it often passes unnoticed. A prevalent mental scheme Quine deems guilty of this error and so worthy of attack is what he calls the "myth of the museum."

In this false view, a conceptual scheme is imaged as a museum in which "the exhibits are meanings and the words are labels."[41] The walls of this museum are not defined by any individual's mental experience, since a conceptual scheme, like most museums, is a public trust rather than private property. Like standing exhibits in a museum, meanings in this conceptual scheme are taken to be part of a permanent collection with an independent reality and value of their own. Having achieved enough recognition to be fixed to the museum's walls, these meanings merit labels of their own so that they can be identified and discussed by those who walk the museum's halls. In Quine's analogy there are in principle as many sets of labels as there are languages. But no matter which particular set of labels identifies the exhibits, no matter which words of an actual language name the meanings, the myth of the museum presupposes words to be funded by their meanings in the conceptual scheme, as though meanings, like museum exhibits, possessed an objectivity capable of appreciation, contemplation, and criticism, whether words are attached to them or not.

The myth of the museum distributes its foundationalism throughout the idea of a conceptual scheme in which meanings are thought to have a mental life of their own apart from their use and applicability in language. If language is born as Quine believes in the practical, ad hoc, and habitual alignment of words to sensory stimulations, then there can be no privileged mental meanings that provide foundations for expression in language. And, a fortiori, there can be no conceptual scheme like the illusory museum that houses independent meanings, however they be described. For Quine, concept-formation cannot be separated from language-formation and so a conceptual scheme can be intelligible only as a product of meaning as use. The museum myth, however, must be rejected not only because it distorts adequate notions of language, concept, and meaning but also because it exaggerates the capabilities of theoretical explanation. Within the museum myth, theories are readily conceived as universal explanations, since the meanings for which they account are believed to be fixed in the mind. The theorist, proceeding from the assumptions of the myth, seeks language that allows meanings to be truthfully translated from the conceptual scheme to language, and from one theoretical explanation to another. In this view, theorizing is successful when its explanations do justice to the conceptual scheme and the objects it frames. But if the myth of the museum is a terribly inadequate (albeit compelling) picture of how meaning works, then deductive theorizing, which flourishes in fixed-meaning conceptual schemes, is equally inadequate. The rejection of the myth of the museum entails the rejection of theory understood as determinate translation from meaning to language.

A theory, for Quine, is simply sentences, "the primary repository of meaning," which offer explanations of how meaning functions semantically.[42] The myth of the museum may encourage, indeed demand, a view of theorizing as a transcendental act of universal translation, but Quine insists that meaning is always provincial. Reference is "nonsense except relative to a coordinate system," one in which use in language provides the only context for meaning. In this view, which Quine describes as "ontological relativity,"[43] meaning is not a transcendental commodity inherent in objects or apprehended in context-free theories. Meaning is a function of context and immanent within it. For Quine, the context of meaning as use finally *is* theory, and we can only "speak from within a theory, albeit any of various."[44] If there is no extra-theoretic truth, then theorizing is not the translation of determinate or fixed meaning. The rootedness of meaning in language-use and the rootedness of language-use in sensory evidence inexorably lead to the judgment that translation remains indeterminate, tied to circumstances continually shaped by the language-use that theorizing is.

Quine expresses this idea by speaking of the "inscrutability of reference," the inability of a language-context to establish some determinate ground within itself that facilitates the redescription of its meaning in another context. Those for whom theories are meaningful, of course, often seek their translation for one reason or another. Quine supports such efforts, as long as they do not proceed from the assumptions of the museum myth. "Translation," he argues,

> is not the recapturing of some determinate entity, a meaning, but only a balancing of various values. An observation sentence and its translation should command assent under similar [sense] stimulations; here is one value. Wide concomitance of assent to standing sentences [observation sentences in spatio-temporal coordinates] is also a value. Good translation strikes some optimum combination of values, insofar as they can be compared.[45]

Quine, then, regards translation as a process of judging, comparing, and assessing relative values within different theoretical settings in order to offer tentative estimations of their relationships. A consequence of this view of translation is that the translated theory is thoroughly enmeshed in both its original and targeted contexts. Inseparable from each, the translation possesses no fixity of its own, but is yet another instance of the scientific endeavor of conceptual bridging between sensory stimulations. This endeavor can never be completed since science remains, in Quine's words, "empirically under-determined." The hypotheses that it proposes are never the only explanations of the available empirical evidence.

Theorists in all disciplines, however, are often insensitive to these natural limitations on their enterprise. A common misunderstanding of theories regards them as fully interpreted sentences, as determinate explanations of their subject matter. The contextuality of theories, however, precludes the possibility of such determinate theoretical explanation. Theories are always located in ever-widening language contexts that become wider still through acts of appropriate translation. Quine expresses this idea in what has come to be known variously as the holism thesis or the Duhem-Quine thesis. According to this position, parts of theories, that is, scientific statements, are "not separately vulnerable to adverse observations, because it is only jointly as a theory that they imply their observable consequences."[46] One might think that contradictory empirical evidence would invalidate the theory with which it clashes. But such an expectation betrays a foundationalist regard for theoretical explanation in which a theory is seen as a compilation of fully interpreted sentences that in their completeness stand or fall together.

For Quine, theoretical explanations are layered, sentence upon sentence and use upon use, so that conflicting observational data need not at all subvert their relative integrity. Our "statements about the external world," he maintains, "face the tribunal of sense experience not individually but only as a corporate body."[47] Indeed, nonconforming or even contradictory data will much more likely have a rippling effect throughout the whole theory, resulting in the revision for which the conflicting evidence calls and of which the theory is constantly in need. Parts of theories are partial explanations in a theory's web of meaning, inseparably related to the background beliefs that define their larger context. But faithfulness to Quine's doctrine of holism means that background beliefs to parts of theories are, from another perspective, parts of theories themselves and only meaningful in relation to background beliefs of their own.

This suggests an infinite regress in the network of justifying beliefs for any theoretical explanation, a prospect only troubling for those who expect a theoretical structure to be based on a foundation of certainty. "However," Quine comments, "such scruples against circularity have little point once we have stopped dreaming of deducing science from observations."[48] In actual practice, "we end the regress of background languages, in discussions of reference, by acquiescing in our mother tongue and taking its words at face value."[49] This course of action provides something like a base in the world of common sense that allows a pragmatic resolution to the problem of the infinite regress, but such a practical stance is quite different from the attempt to end the infinite regress by positing a certain foundation within theoretical explanation itself. Recourse to foundationalist theories necessarily falls prey to the museum myth, seeks to escape the naturalistic setting in which epistemology is rightly at home, and contradicts the noetic and ontological relativity that a naturalistic epistemology implies.

Both Sellars and Quine reject the Cartesian heritage unwittingly embraced in assumptions about how we know by articulating and undermining the mental myths authoritatively invoked to justify theoretical explanation. In the work of Richard Rorty we meet another attempt to expose the illusion of foundations for knowing by considering the metaphorical appeal of such an assumption. Rorty, though, takes the history of philosophy, rather than the logical framework of theories, as his investigative field.

Seeing the Truth: Rorty on Metaphors and Foundations

Richard Rorty's self-understanding as a philosopher might best be described as subversive. Like Sellars and Quine, he refuses to recognize the traditional disciplinary integrity of philosophy, insisting with his nonfoundational colleagues that philosophy is continuous with science. Any traditional regard for philosophy as an enterprise with its own special problems, business, and modus operandi would entail a commitment to metaphysical assumptions that Rorty believes have run their historical course and shown themselves to be meaningless. The view that philosophy is a discipline independent from "science," broadly speaking, would make no sense whatsoever "without the Cartesian claim that by turning inward we could find ineluctable truth, and the Kantian claim that this truth imposes limits on the possible results of empirical inquiry." Rorty's project is to subvert this epistemological tradition by attacking belief "in the 'mind' as something about which one should have a 'philosophical' view, in 'knowledge' as something about which there ought to be a 'theory' and which has 'foundations,' and in 'philosophy' as it has been conceived since Kant."⁵⁰

In *Philosophy and the Mirror of Nature* (1979), Rorty commences this deconstructive project by explaining just how the Western philosophical tradition has come to be enamored of the idea of foundations for knowledge. Western philosophers from Plato to Kant, Rorty argues, usually have distinguished between the mental and the physical worlds in framing the problem of knowing. Whether rationalists or empiricists configured the mental world, they posited its experience as a grounding for any knowledge that claimed to be genuine. In this noetic schematism, thinking (or experiencing) is regarded as an activity that mirrors reality, presenting its truth immediately and firsthand within its very operations. Whether traditional philosophy portrayed reality and its truth as supersensible ideas, the objects of sense impressions, or the thing-in-itself, its privileging of some dimension of mental life as a direct, epistemic avenue to that reality took shape in the assumption that knowledge must have foundations to support the greater share of epistemic claims incapable themselves of direct and immediate validation.

This sweeping assessment of the traditional metaphysical tradition might have been offered by any of Rorty's nonfoundational precursors and colleagues considered thus far. Among Rorty's special contributions to this general critique are his attention to the role of metaphor in fostering commitment to metaphysical assumptions and his efforts to redefine the philosophical task as exposing the intrinsic foundationalism of the Cartesian heritage.

Redefining Philosophy

In Rorty's view, foundationalist epistemologies are merely sophisticated variants of fundamentalism. Much in the manner of unquestioning political and religious allegiances, their attractiveness lies in their promise of ready answers, the banishing of doubt in absolute certainty, and membership in a coterie of true believers. Specifically, the appeal of foundationalist epistemologies lies in their common expectation that an immediate experience establishes the truthful certainty of other claims in the system of knowledge. To the degree that their interlocutors or readers accept the self-certainty of the particular dimension of immediacy privileged in their respective positions, foundationalist philosophers attract a bevy of like-minded adherents for whom careful epistemic justification is rendered superfluous. For those willing to embrace the foundationalist view of knowledge, truths are regarded as "certain because of their causes rather than because of the arguments given for them."[51] However airy or earthy such a causal first principle may be, the foundationalist's belief in the revelatory power of its self-evident truth leads to what Rorty calls a "confrontationalist epistemology," a theory of knowledge in which visual metaphors often and unconsciously have encouraged the foundationalist error.

Ocular imagery, Rorty argues, was first invoked by the ancient Greeks to convey an essentially contemplative understanding of human thought's encounter with truth. Plato conceived of philosophical contemplation as an act in which the veridical foundations of knowledge could be reached "by escaping from the senses and opening up the faculty of reason—the Eye of the Soul—to the World of Being."[52] The force of such imagery, Rorty points out, is that it patterns the mind's beholding truth on the immediacy of visual experience in which nothing intervenes between the workings of the optic nerve and the splashings of light upon the world of objects. This "spectator" epistemology assumes that an objective truth causes subjective dispositions of certainty much in the way that light's configuration of the outside world "causes" the stimulations of visual experience, and that the immediate interface between subjectivity and objectivity constitutes the foundations that all acts of knowing presuppose.

Variations on the theme of visual confrontation continued to be played in the Western metaphysical tradition well beyond Plato's first appeal to this analogy for philosophical insight. Descartes believed reasoning to be based on epistemic foundations which were indubitable and to which credible alternatives could not be posited when "the Eye of the Mind [turned] from the confused inner representations to the clear and distinct ones."[53] For Locke, the "seeing" of sense experience brought the objective world into direct contact with human awareness and defined foundations for knowledge that were less reflexive than Descartes's, though no less immediate in character. Kant sought a "transcendental standpoint outside our present set of representations from which we can inspect the relations between those representations and their object,"[54] a mental position imaged as a viewing stand from which the parade of sense experience is examined and ordered according to the subjective judge's a priori program.

In all of these influential strategies—whether ancient or modern, rationalist or empiricist—ocular imagery conveys the experiential immediacy that, it is assumed, alone can resist the incursions of doubt and relativity. Rorty insists that there is nothing sacrosanct about such imagery. It is as arbitrary as the foundationalist assumptions it seeks to express.[55] Indeed, one of the most striking theses of *Philosophy and the Mirror of Nature* is its claim that the very notion of "the mind" that contemporary philosophers are wont to find at issue in the work of philosophers throughout the ages is actually an invention of the post-Cartesian tradition. In this modern construction of epistemological categories, the mind came to be conceived as "an inner space in which both pains and clear and distinct ideas passed in review before a single Inner Eye," and "indubitability," the mind's certainty, gradually replaced eternity as a "criterion of the mental."[56]

According to Rorty, this invention of the mind as the seat of veridical authority extended the perceived need for foundations for knowledge to the discipline of philosophy itself, and gave rise to the modern, Cartesian preoccupation with epistemology. As the mind was vested with extraordinary authority, philosophy came to be understood as the discipline that explains not only how knowledge is acquired but also, and more importantly, how the workings of the mind enable that acquisition. "Philosophy," Rorty states, "became 'primary' no longer in the sense of 'highest' but in the sense of 'underlying.' "[57] Its practitioners expected it to be nothing less than a foundational discipline, a necessary propaedeutic for all the disciplines in its task of locating the possibility of knowledge itself in the mirror of nature that modern epistemologists believed the mind to be.

For Rorty, the invention of the mind as the measure of certainty and the grandiose definition of philosophy as the basis of culture heightened the traditional desire for foundational immediacy. In his revisionist narrative of Western philosophy, Rorty judges this Cartesian desire to be nothing less than tyrannous. The yearning for foundational immediacy expects that reality will be "unveiled to us, not as in a glass darkly, but with some unimaginable sort of immediacy which would make discourse and description superfluous."[58] The dialogue that Rorty believes authentic philosophizing to be is despotically silenced in the desire for foundational certainty. In his more democratic conception of the philosophical enterprise this dialogue would not be stifled by the foundationalist assertion of first principles but would unfold in a multitude of voices, none presumptuous enough to think that its experience or words could bring the dialogue to closure.

Edifying Philosophy

Hermeneutics is Rorty's prescription for the philosophical malady of epistemology. Conversation, and not construction, is the only legitimate course for philosophers to take who want to avoid the vanity of foundationalism. Hermeneutics, for Rorty, is not another philosophical project, a program with its own agenda, rules, and purposes standing ready to succeed traditional epistemology. It "is an expression of hope that the cultural space left by the demise of epistemology will not be filled—that our culture should become one in which the demand for constraint and confrontation is no longer felt."[59] Hermeneutics is not another method but a philosophical style committed to the ongoing exchange of views about what is meaningful in lives, disciplines, and cultures. The philosophical task so conceived, Rorty proposes, would be a "way of coping,"[60] a promising therapy not only for the disciplinary illness of epistemology but also for the very insecurities of human life that philosophy has sought to soothe since ancient times.

This, in Rorty's term, "edifying" approach to the philosophical task would relinquish the Cartesian tradition's systematic aspirations for foundations for knowledge and also stand on guard against the pretensions of "confrontationist" philosophy, whether they appear in their more traditional forms or in latter-day varieties of rationalism or empiricism. An edifying philosophy would set a negative agenda for the philosophical enterprise. It would renounce the value of any philosophy seeking a common denominator for epistemic translation. It would expose the philosophical inadequacy of visual metaphors and the authority of experiential immediacy they convey. And it would forsake the traditional understanding of philosophy as a research project in search of truth. Even though Rorty portrays edifying philosophy as "reactive" and as "having sense only as a protest" against foundationalist philosophy,[61] there are a number of respects in which its approach can be described in positive, even if not in constructive, terms.

In the pages of *Philosophy and the Mirror of Nature*, and also in his more recent *Contingency, Irony, and Solidarity* (1989), Rorty sketches his understanding of what a nonfoundational philosophy would be. First and foremost, an edifying philosophy would be modest in its aspirations for what philosophy could achieve in its search for meaning in the human condition. It would recognize the radical temporality of knowledge and its boundedness to the cultural contexts which produce it. What the foundationalist would define pejoratively as epistemic relativism, Rorty prefers to describe as the existential contingencies of language, selfhood, and community which the nonfoundational philosopher—to say nothing of human beings—must embrace rather than repress.[62]

An edifying philosophy is an exercise in redescribing our customary assumptions, ideas, and commitments in terms that break the foundationalist mold traditionally set for them. Such an approach resists the grandiose projects of theorists like G. W. F. Hegel, Friedrich Nietzsche, and Martin Heidegger who, Rorty coyly notes, respectively offered descriptions of nothing less than "Spirit," "Europe," and "Being" itself. An edifying philosopher adopts the pose of the ironist, a "person who faces up to the contingency of his or her own most central beliefs and desires," and in describing the human condition follows the novelist's lead in attending to circumstance, dilemma, and detail.[63] Such a description, Rorty claims, would produce an "abnormal" discourse, one that breaks from the foundational conventions of grand narratives and universal theories and that, unlike these metaphysical modes of discourse, is committed to the open-ended meaning of the sustained conversation.

Wisdom, in Rorty's view, is the ability to sustain a cultural conversation that resists the fundamentalist desire for closure, for only through such a conversation can the hope for communal solidarity be realized. Moral obligation, he thinks, is all too easily co-opted when conceived as responsibility to objective principles dwelling in a hypostatized human conscience. Liberal aspirations for justice have a far greater chance of satisfaction when commitment to them is ventured on smaller scales, within the cultural, national, ethnic, or even neighborhood communities in which edifying discourse can be conducted and in which the more local identifications required to support action for justice are possible.[64]

In this regard, Rorty understands more to be at stake in the criticism of foundationalism than simply the correction of a logical error, of interest only to professional philosophers. His edifying or nonfoundational approach to critical discourse includes among its responsibilities pragmatic commitment to the betterment of human beings in the communities in which they live. A Cartesian may wonder how such commitment can be made, since the conditions of its possibility have not first been established. The absence of foundations, though, is no deterrent to commitment as long as we adjust our conception of what that commitment does and does not presuppose to be enacted. Vision, in Rorty's judgment, may not supply satisfying images for this or any other legitimate understanding of the philosophical task. Were we to look to one of the other five senses for an appropriate metaphor to convey his expectations of an edifying or nonfoundational philosophy, it would be hearing or, more specifically, the listening that Rorty prizes so highly in his view of philosophical conversation rightly conducted.

Justifying Belief

Our brief forays into the thought of Sellars, Quine, and Rorty have exhibited a diversity in the way contemporary philosophers attack the idea of foundations for knowledge. In their dissatisfaction with the premise that knowledge possesses an authoritative ground, nonfoundational philosophers defend a particular understanding of the task of justifying belief. One might say that all philosophical explanations—from the simplest logical syllogism to the grandest metaphysical claims—are exercises in justifying belief. Philosophical explanations attempt to provide sufficient reasons for holding particular assumptions, arguing in specific directions, and reaching reasoned conclusions. The foundationalist, however, begins from the presupposition that offering sufficient reasons for knowledge finally depends on the existence of beliefs that, though justifying others, require no justification themselves.

For the foundationalist, this "originary" belief may be anchored in sense experience or ideas or the structure of the mind. Whatever its provenance, what matters to the foundationalist is that the belief be noninferential, that it *not* be posed as a defensible consequence of belief for which credible explanations have been given. If all knowledge is inferential, if all its claims take the form of justified beliefs, then, the foundationalist argues, none of its claims can finally assuage the doubt and uncertainty that prompt justificatory explanation in the first place. Foundationalist approaches to philosophy insist that the very possibility of knowing depends on there being a noninferential basis for justified belief, a "ground" or "foundation" whose apparent certainty can warrant claims in the larger edifice of inferential knowledge and so enable the justification of belief. Were one to follow the nonfoundation-alist in denying the need for such noninferential beliefs, the result, the foundationalist fears, would be a relativism so thorough that genuine acts of knowing would be nothing more than vain hopes and philosophical justification of any sort a logical impossibility.

Cartesian Anxiety

In his important book *Beyond Objectivism and Relativism* (1983), Richard Bernstein comments on this foundationalist fear with much acumen. Contemporary philosophers, Bernstein observes, are polarized into rival camps defined by their commitment to the positions of "objectivism" and "relativism." Objectivism is "the basic conviction that there is or must be some permanent, ahistorical matrix or framework to which we can ultimately appeal in determining the nature of rationality, knowledge, truth, reality, goodness, or rightness." Objectivism is "closely related to foundationalism," its adherents maintaining against relativists that "unless we can ground philosophy, knowledge, or language in a rigorous manner we cannot avoid radical skepticism."[65] Bernstein considers this position to be as stereotypical and untenable as the relativism by which it is supposedly threatened, and questions why it has been so prevalent in the history of philosophy. Objectivist expectations of knowledge, he suggests, are expressions of the Western philosophical tradition's "Cartesian anxiety," the debilitating epistemic worry that without foundations knowledge can in fact be no more than opinion, itself completely vulnerable to doubt and skepticism.[66] — *and to will and vote*

Bernstein does not wish to identify the "Cartesian anxiety" exclusively with the thought and heritage of Descartes. Concern about the encroachments of relativism are as old as the Platonic quest for truth beyond time and culture. But, in Bernstein's view, no philosopher in the modern period, or in any period for that matter, has articulated the foundationalist fear more clearly than Descartes, for whom the relationship between objectivism and relativism stood as a dichotomous either/or. This disjunctive estimation of their disciplinary alternatives is, for Descartes and his followers, simply a choice between the possibility and the impossibility of the philosophical task. Either knowledge possesses objective foundations, the Cartesians claim, and can be grounded in secure and stable truth, or it lacks foundations and is nothing more than a relativistic assemblage of unreliable viewpoints.

Philosophy, Cartesians maintain, can distinguish between mere thinking and founded knowing only if an evaluative norm is accessible to the mind. In the absence of such a criterion, philosophical justification would be directionless and pointless. From a historical perspective, the Cartesian anxiety expresses the traditional privileging of the objectivist position in the history of Western philosophy, its modern uneasiness all the more keen as philosophy's explanatory power has waned in the present century with the rise of pragmatic and contextual approaches to the philosophical task. But in the more rarefied setting of logic, there is no better illustration of what causes the foundationalist's "Cartesian anxiety" than the prospect of an infinite regress in the order of justifying belief.

An Infinite Regress?

The advantage foundationalists find in an objectivist approach to philosophy is that its assumptions allow the task of justifying belief to be, at least in principle, feasible. The many conceptions of foundations in the history of philosophy may testify to the difficulty involved in settling on authentic, epistemic grounds. But in strictly logical terms, foundations seem to be necessary to objectivists if the task of justifying belief is to be carried out. In the absence of foundations, the objectivist argues, the task of justifying belief would lead to an infinite regress in the logic of justification. If beliefs sought justification by appealing for their authority only to justified beliefs that in turn appealed for their authority only to justified beliefs, and so on, then, the foundationalist fears, the logical possibility of there being epistemic authority at all would be abolished.

William Alston has argued against a nonfoundational conception of justifying belief by raising the specter of the infinite regress. If foundations for knowledge do not exist, then justification would take place, as the nonfoundationalist claims, only in a network of mutually supportive beliefs. But, Alston argues, this approach would result either in an infinite regress in justification (in which justificatory conclusions could never be reached) or in a completely circular begging of the question (the very problem that philosophical justification aims to redress).[67] Whether working foundations for knowledge can actually be demonstrated is less important to Alston than establishing the logical *viability* of foundationalism, for the reasonable possibility of noninferential belief, Alston thinks, would be sufficient to halt the spiral of the infinite regress, and thus establish the possibility of any and every act of knowing.

It would not be difficult to anticipate how the nonfoundational philosophers considered thus far would respond to the infinite regress argument. Rather than return to the philosophies of Sellars, Quine, and Rorty for rejoinders, though, we will consider the counterarguments of two other defenders of the nonfoundational position, Donald Davidson and Michael Williams.

Donald Davidson's influential essay, "On the Very Idea of a Conceptual Scheme," probes the boundaries of conceptual schemes, like cultures, worldviews, or personal beliefs, to determine how one might distinguish among different schemes or define the particulars of one's own. Davidson's reflections on this topic do not directly address the problem of the infinite justificatory regress, although they do have interesting implications for this issue. A conceptual scheme, he claims, can be thought of as a language, though "speakers of different languages may share a conceptual scheme provided there is a way of translating one language into the other."[68] At its widest expanse, a conceptual scheme can be understood as intertranslatable languages. Acts of translation may enable a conceptual scheme to extend beyond particular languages. But such acts, Davidson notes, can only be accomplished within a conceptual scheme, and so evince the assumptions, perspectives, and values of the scheme. "There is," he maintains, "no chance that someone can take up a vantage point for comparing conceptual schemes by temporarily shedding his own."[69] Philosophical pragmatists would regard the idea that truth is relative to a conceptual scheme as a truism, as a claim for little more than the obvious. Davidson's analysis, however, shows this truism to be a richer source of philosophical insight than it initially might appear.

If intertranslatable languages present a conceptual scheme writ large, and no evaluative perspective exists outside conceptual schemes, then the notion of a radically different conceptual scheme is unintelligible. A radically different conceptual scheme could only be discerned through an utter failure in translation. But an untranslatable scheme, Davidson points out, could only be recognized from a neutral, objective position that would by definition stand outside language, and so outside thought, and so outside the human.[70] Such a standpoint, an evaluative foundation we might say, simply does not exist:

> Neither a fixed stock of meanings, nor a theory-neutral reality, can provide, then, a ground for comparison of conceptual schemes. It would be a mistake to look further for such a ground if by that we mean something conceived as common to incommensurable schemes. In abandoning this search, we abandon the attempt to make sense of the metaphor of a single space within which each scheme has a position and provides a point of view.[71]

The extreme case of the untranslatable, and so unintelligible, conceptual scheme has important consequences for defining the boundaries of any conceptual scheme at all. For if conceptual schemes can be judged only intraschematically, within the vast spectrum of intertranslatable languages, then there is finally no way of marking the difference between one conceptual scheme and another. It would be possible in principle to identify schematic boundaries if the form of a conceptual scheme were distinguishable from its content. Such a distinction between form and content, however, could only be made from a neutral standpoint outside the conceptual scheme, a requirement that violates the most basic truism about the schematic relativity of any position. Since a conceptual scheme is as large as intertranslatable languages, its meaning is a vastly proliferating network within which a schematic "form" could not be differentiated from a schematic "content." In other words, the boundaries of a conceptual scheme extend to infinity.

At first glance this conclusion seems to imply the most open-armed ecumenism in the order of conceptual schemes. If there is no way to set the boundaries of a conceptual scheme "from without" by virtue of the unintelligibility of an untranslatable conceptual scheme, and no way to determine schematic boundaries even "from within" by virtue of the indeterminable extension of intertranslatable languages, then Davidson seems to suggest that all possible conceptual schemes are one. This judgment, he claims, is unwarranted. "For we have found no intelligible basis on which it can be said that schemes are different . . . [and] if we cannot intelligibly say that schemes are different, neither can we intelligibly say that they are one."[72] Any schematic boundaries, even the boundaries implied in the idea of an utterly comprehensive schematic unity, could only be determined from a foundationalist, extraschematic perspective that, Davidson concludes, is an epistemic illusion.

As we have noted, Davidson's reflections on conceptual schemes are not directly offered as a rejoinder to the foundationalist fear of the infinite regress, but they do much to put that fear in perspective. The foundationalist poses the problem of the infinite regress as a threat to the very possibility of philosophical justification, as though authoritative warrants for any belief could not occur without the postulation of an immediately justified justifying belief. Davidson's stance on the impossibility of differentiating conceptual schemes, however, suggests that the foundationalist's "Cartesian anxiety" is, in his opinion, more accurately diagnosed as epistemological agoraphobia. The foundationalist fears the utterly open spaces of a boundless conceptual (or more explicitly, justificatory) scheme, for its ever-receding horizon—imaged as an infinite regress of justification—seems to vitiate the very possibility of philosophical explanation. The foundationalist, one could say, arbitrarily draws a boundary where none could possibly exist and designates that boundary as the foundation, the epistemic sine qua non, for what is now mistakenly regarded as a differentiated or finite scheme of justification.

The boundless character of a conceptual scheme need not lead one to despair about the possibility of justifying belief. Philosophical justification can still take place in the indeterminate setting of all intertranslatable languages, even if it eschews the task of establishing the possibility of truth within a finite conceptual scheme. Justification in this manner would involve assessing the adequacy of our sentences or theories to our experience, a task that would be as continuous, as revisable, and as interpreted as the languages in which our sentences and theories take shape. Davidson would be untroubled by justification so conceived, and even offers the assurance that philosophical explanation can still hold to the notion of objective truth. "Of course," he wryly observes, the "truth of sentences remains relative to language, but that is as objective as can be."[73]

Open-Ended Explanation

A rejoinder to the infinite regress argument is explicitly developed by Michael Williams in his book *Groundless Belief* (1977). Williams sympathizes with the foundationalist concern for justifying belief as an expression of the age-old philosophical desire to distinguish genuine knowledge from mere opinion. The foundationalist, however, defines the task of justification in opposition to the alternative and unhappy prospect of an infinite regress in philosophical explanation. An infinite regress in justifying belief would multiply opinion endlessly, never reach a finally authoritative claim, and so lack the foundation needed to imbue its explanation with authority. The justification of belief, the foundationalist expects, must be finite if justification is to be possible at all. Williams does not find this argument convincing. In actual practice, he observes, justifying belief is inevitably a finite process. But the fact that justification ends does not warrant the claim for a foundation on which knowledge necessarily rests. A finite regress requires only that "at any given time we must have some stock of beliefs which are not thought to be open to challenge, though any one of them may come under fire." In any case, Williams asserts, it would be "clearly fallacious to argue that, since justification must come to an end somewhere, there must be some special kind of belief with which justification always terminates."[74]

Since foundationalists regard an infinite regress in explanation as inconsistent with the philosophical task, they often enlist its threat as an argument for the logical consistency of their own approach to justification. In Williams's judgment, the infinite justificatory regress is perceived as threatening only in light of a "genetic" conceptualization of how knowledge is acquired. Foundationalists maintain that the entire epistemic system must have a first belief, or at least basic beliefs, if any act of knowing can be warranted. But this genetic view of knowledge is based on two assumptions that cannot be validated. First, foundationalists assume that justification requires a unique beginning in a foundational belief different from all others. Second, they expect that "every evidential connexion must hold either inductively or else analytically," that the authority of a foundational belief as a matter of course would be efficacious throughout the whole network of justified belief.[75] These assumptions may be understandable hopes, but they are not logically defensible.

Against the foundationalist position, Williams would define the task of epistemology as "accommodating beliefs that are being questioned to a body of accepted beliefs,"[76] rather than as a search for the origins of knowledge. Like Davidson, he understands philosophical justification as a process that is open-ended and modest in what it counts as success. Philosophical explanation, Williams concedes, must end somewhere since it, like all human activities, is limited by time and circumstance. Nothing other than time and circumstance, though, can bring justification to closure. Its ending is relative, and quickly reversible as soon as philosophical talent puts its abilities back to work. In Williams's words, justification "always terminates with other *beliefs* and not with our confronting 'raw chunks of reality,' for that idea is incoherent."[77]

Williams concludes that the infinite justificatory regress is not the threat the foundationalist takes it to be. The foundationalist may be convinced that the absence of privileged grounds for knowledge in an infinite regress makes the philosophical task impossible. What the foundationalist defines as the very possibility of the philosophical task, however, is actually a particular, and logically dubious, conception of its possibility. The foundationalist expects that justifying belief requires the authority of noninferential belief if the authority of the whole system of knowledge is to be established. But this assumption exhibits the foundationalist longing for a scheme of knowledge with clear and distinct boundaries in which the justification of belief can be brought to absolute closure. On the one hand, Williams claims, no evidence in experience or in the task of justification suggests that bodies of knowledge are bounded in any way or that a nonfoundational approach to justification would subvert itself. On the other hand, he thinks, the foundationalist's understanding of knowledge, justification, and epistemic authority is supported by such a large number of unwarranted assumptions that there is little, if anything, to justify belief in foundations.

In his recent book *Pursuit of Truth* (1990), Quine describes himself as a member of that "large minority or small majority who repudiate the Cartesian dream of a foundation for scientific certainty firmer than scientific method itself."[78] Were we to count philosophers who repudiate the Cartesian dream for reasons other than Quine's, we would certainly have to revise his playful description of advocates of nonfoundationalism by fixing their plurality as a large majority. That nonfoundational criticism is now practiced by a majority of contemporary philosophers testifies to the cogency of its analysis, the adequacy of its explanation, and its consistency with experience. As we shall see in the next chapter, a number of contemporary theologians also have embraced nonfoundational philosophy as a critical resource for interpretation in their own discipline. It is to their proposals for a nonfoundational theology that we now turn.

2

Nonfoundationalism and Modern Theology

S uch a diversity of themes, approaches, and methods char-
acterizes the history of theology that any number of perspectives could serve as compasses to chart the course of this
discipline through the ages. One could consider, for example,
the history of theology in terms of the interests of various schools
of thought whose concerns have appeared and reappeared in
different eras. Or one could map the history of theology as a host
of qualified commitments to either theoretical or practical styles
of reflection. Or one could view the same history as the history
of the interpretation of scripture, or as the speaking and writing
that fosters the development of doctrine, or as the practice of
changing understandings of theological responsibility. One common way of charting the historical course of theology is by considering its relationship to the discipline of philosophy. From this
viewpoint, theology presents itself as a discipline configured by
its association with particular philosophical systems whose rational accounts of human existence in the world shed new light
on the meaning of the gospel.

There are several reasons for the prevalence of this last perspective as a way of appreciating the history of theology. The
traditional Augustinian definition of theology as faith seeking
understanding readily welcomes theology's self-definition in relation to philosophy. To the degree that faith seeks understanding
that is ordered and not inchoate, it is often drawn to available
systems of thought whose coherence presents a structure for the

interpretation of scripture and ecclesial tradition. Another reason might be that histories of disciplines lend themselves to the traditional preference for the history of ideas. As an ancient and theoretical discipline itself, theology is easily situated in a long history of the compelling philosophical ideas that have defined Western culture from the metaphysical age of pre-Enlightenment to the critical age of post-Enlightenment culture.

The strongest reason for marking the history of theology in terms of its relationship to philosophy is that most Christian theologians, directly or indirectly, actually have appealed to philosophical ideas, explanations, and worldviews in order to convey their religious insights. Justin Martyr's and Augustine's uses of Platonism, Aquinas's employment of Aristotelian categories, Luther's appeal to the worldview of late medieval nominalism, Schleiermacher's commitment to the experiential psychology of German idealism, Bultmann's appreciation of Heidegger's existentialism, and Gustavo Gutiérrez's use of Marxist analysis are just a few of the many examples one could cite of theological attempts to find guides for the illumination of faith in philosophical positions. If the history of theology can be charted by the compass of philosophical reflection, it is because such reflection has played an important role in its history, one so important, in fact, that only the most contrived abstraction could distinguish finally between the history of theology and the philosophical influences upon it.

Philosophies, then, have long provided a context for theological reflection without which the history of theology would look unimaginably different. As philosophical explanations gain currency in their own times they are often judged by theologians to elucidate the church's experience of redemption and to provide means for conveying the relevance of its message within a particular climate of understanding. Were the history of theology to serve as evidence, theologians of every generation would be seen to have turned to the philosophies of their day for epistemologies, metaphysics, and anthropologies able to articulate the claims about the drama of human salvation that are definitively Christian.

Viewed in light of this history, the interpretive possibilities of nonfoundational philosophy for theological reflection seem remarkably limited, if not completely empty. Nonfoundational philosophies are consistently critical of the epistemologies, metaphysics, and anthropologies that premodern and modern philosophers have offered as the defensible consequences of reasoning. Foundationalist philosophers present their conclusions as inferences drawn from allegedly noninferential beliefs that in turn are assumed to provide sure and secure foundations for human knowledge. As we have seen, thinkers like Willard Quine, Wilfred Sellars, Richard Rorty, and Donald Davidson take this assumption to task, arguing that justifying belief is an endless task that neither possesses nor requires epistemic foundations to establish the possibility of meaningful inquiry. Nonfoundational philosophies, then, undermine the classical and modern styles of philosophical reflection on which theology consistently has relied in its own constructive efforts.

If the history of theology is inextricably bound to philosophical positions that are foundational in character, then it seems that that same history also would be guilty of foundationalism. Theologies that advance their arguments by inference from unsubstantiated metaphysical principles could only be judged logically deficient from a nonfoundational standpoint. Moreover, the discipline of theology itself seems in large part to have invested the possibility of its knowledge in philosophies that nonfoundational criticism has shown to be based on unwarranted assumptions. Theology, from these perspectives, is guilty on two counts before the court of nonfoundational criticism: its argumentation tainted by questionable philosophical premises and its disciplinary integrity subverted by its appeal to foundational construals of theoretical explanation.

Perhaps, though, we could concede more than we have so far to our imaginative powers and entertain the possibility of theologies that reach conclusions without relying foundationally on the whole or the parts of particular philosophies. Even though such theologies would avoid the most typical and obvious foundationalist pitfall, they would still, I suggest, be subject to the nonfoundational critique. As different as nonfoundational philosophies may be in labeling the impediments to legitimate philosophical explanation and in redefining its proper conduct, all argue that no authoritative givenness exists in experience or in reasoning from which philosophical explanation may infer legitimate conclusions. But this attack on the viability of authoritative foundations is as consequential for theological as it is for philosophical reasoning.

Theological claims are reasoned attempts to understand the authoritative givenness of God's revelation in scripture or in the sanctioned tradition of its interpretation through the ages. Theology assumes (or might we better say believes?) that the authoritative givenness of the gospel provides an indispensable basis for its reflection, in philosophical terminology a justifying belief which itself is incapable of justification. Indeed, the classical Augustinian definition of theology as faith seeking understanding subordinates rational inquiry to the given authority of faith in God's revelation. Theology seems to be a discipline shaped by epistemological commitments that most contemporary philosophers would identify as blatantly foundational, and so susceptible through and through to the nonfoundational critique. As the Cartesian philosopher appeals to clear and distinct ideas, or the Humean to the immediacy of sense impressions, or the Kantian to the seemingly unassailable truth of a priori knowledge, the Christian theologian appeals in faith to the truth of divine revelation, and theological reasoning proceeds in any number of ways from the authority of this immediately justified belief.

Can, then, theology embrace a philosophical position like nonfoundationalism? Our analysis so far seems to suggest a negative answer to this question. On the one hand, the nonfoundational critique of knowledge seems to vitiate theology's traditional practice of employing philosophical explanations, often foundationalist stances themselves, as grounds for theological inquiry. On the other hand, and of even greater consequence, the nonfoundational critique seems to extend to the most fundamental authoritative claims of theology itself, apart from which theology—at least Christian theology—would simply lose its identity. Nonfoundational philosophers are confident that their discipline can be reconfigured to serve a useful purpose in our postmetaphysical age. Christian theologians, however, could have no such hope for their discipline if its nonfoundational revision entailed the rejection of its authoritative basis in the claims of divine revelation.[1] Nonfoundational criticism and theology seem to represent completely incompatible modes of argumentation and stances on the possibilities, limitations, and authority of human knowing.

Were we to expect the nonfoundational position to be applied theologically in the broadest sense possible, it would be difficult to imagine a fruitful result. We should note, though, that theological applications of any philosophy—whether an epistemology, a metaphysics, a worldview, or a critical stance—are always particular or regional, for any complete application would simply reiterate the philosophical position under consideration and eclipse its specifically theological value. Augustine, for example, made much of Plotinus's understanding of the God-world relationship, even though he did not accept Plotinus's conception of the divine nature as impersonal. Aquinas found Aristotle's categories useful in explaining the identity of essence and existence in God but rejected Aristotle's belief in the eternity of the world. Bultmann found Heidegger's view on human authenticity in the face of death to be a powerful way of expressing Christian commitment, but rejected his claim that the authentic decision is made in an otherwise meaningless context. Nonfoundationalism as a philosophical position may have no substance of its own capable of theological use, and its claims in and of themselves may be the most powerful arguments to surface thus far in the philosophical tradition against the disciplinary integrity of theology. But there are, I would suggest, respects in which the contrariness of nonfoundational criticism can be put to the service of theology.

As we have seen in the previous chapter, nonfoundational criticism presents sophisticated arguments against the logical viability of foundationalist reasoning. As a hermeneutics of suspicion, it exposes the naiveté of the very assumptions by which the Western intellectual tradition often marks its identity. Nonfoundational criticism checks the pretensions toward rationalist or empiricist speculation characteristic of classical metaphysics and modern epistemology and underscores the fragility of epistemic claims. Nonfoundational criticism is willing to rethink a discipline's customary obligations in light of its recognition of the contextuality, contingency, and revisability of knowledge. Nonfoundationalism may be incapable of an unqualified theological appropriation. But its critical insights into the nature of knowledge and the practice of reasoning could set courses for theological interpretation as interesting as those pursued in philosophy by Quine, Rorty, and Bernstein.

This chapter considers how nonfoundational sensibilities have informed theological interpretation. Our approach will be thematic and illustrative. After examining how the very notion of modernity is configured from a nonfoundational standpoint, we shall consider the arguments by George Lindbeck and Ronald Thiemann against the apologetical use of foundational theories, Hans Frei's attention to narrative realism as a contextual medium for Christian meaning, and the implications of nonfoundational criticism for the integrity of theological reasoning. These topics do not exhaust the possible issues that nonfoundational theologies might address, nor are they in any way fundamental to the nonfoundational approach. They do present a variety of ways in which theologians implicitly or explicitly have invoked the nonfoundational perspective to clarify the claims of the Christian gospel and their vocational responsibility to foster those claims. If our presentation is successful, the result will be an overview of the concerns and styles of nonfoundational theologies, and a backdrop for considering the critical issues suggested by their interpretive approach.

The Modern Theological Tradition in Nonfoundational Perspective

Those who have advocated a nonfoundational approach to theology often have done so in light of their assessment of the predicament of theology, and for that matter Christianity, in the modern age. There are, of course, many ways of defining the historical parameters of modern theology, as well as its assumptions and tasks. For the purposes of our brief treatment, modern theology refers to nonfundamentalist theology of the post-Enlightenment period. Modern theology may be descriptive, speculative, or critical in its approach, or liberal or conservative in its leanings. But even within the rich pluralism that might itself be named as one of its traits, modern theology has consistently wrestled with its own status as a discipline in the face of the social assumptions and practices the Enlightenment set in place.

Theology after the Enlightenment

As a movement both intellectual and political in scope, the Enlightenment sought the reform of society by proclaiming the dignity and rights of the individual, and to that end denounced the traditional bastions of feudal and religious authority that had been the mainstays of the old order. The Enlightenment could denounce the divine right of kings only by first calling into question the divine revelation on which the very truth-claims of Christianity rested. Invoking the coherence of the Newtonian worldview to denounce the credibility of miracles, Enlightenment thinkers rejected even the possibility of the central salvational acts of Jesus Christ as preposterous absurdities. Drawing on the newly developed historical-critical method, Enlightenment thinkers cited the irreconcilable inconsistencies in scripture as evidence that the sacred text was at best a reasonably defensible collection of moral dictates, at worst poor history, and by no means what the Christian tradition claimed it to be—the divinely revealed Word of God. For the rationalists, the world's coming of age meant that the Christian vision of God, humanity, and society had been superseded by an anthropology of human perfectibility, the achievements of the arts and secular sciences, and the political hopes of the late eighteenth-century revolutions.

Theology, as the reflective interpretation of scripture, could not help but suffer the same consequences of this rationalistic critique of revelation. Some theologians found the new, critical truth to be so compelling that it demanded their commitment and entailed the rejection of the Christianity they had previously affirmed. Others simply ignored its threat to traditional Christianity and continued on in their belief and their work as though the Enlightenment had no truth to tell at all. The directions of modern theology were set by a third group of theologians who embraced the critical spirit of the Enlightenment, shared its concerns about traditional religious authority, and respected its claims for the authority of individual experience, but who believed that such stances could be reconciled with Christianity's fundamental truth-claims. If modernity was represented by the critical spirit of the Enlightenment, then these theologians were unwilling to regard modern theology as a contradiction in terms that demanded the unqualified affirmation of either the adjective or the noun. Friedrich Schleiermacher (1768–1834), one of the first and perhaps the most influential of modern theologians, voiced the unacceptability of this dilemma in a famous rhetorical question posed in his *Open Letters to Dr. Lücke* (1829): "Shall the tangle of history so unravel that Christianity becomes identified with barbarism and science with unbelief?"[2]

Since Schleiermacher's day, generations of post-Enlightenment theologians have confronted the false dilemma of a modern theology by embracing apologetics as a dimension of the theological task itself. Theology, in this typically modern configuration, formulates a method that justifies its disciplinary integrity before the Enlightenment's rigorous canons for legitimate knowledge, and specifies a content that answers the Enlightenment's attacks on Christianity's most central doctrines. Apologetical method at the very least embraces the principles of historical criticism as consistent with the act of reflection by which faith seeks understanding. And theology's apologetical content at the very least offers its exposition of Christian faith aware of the Enlightenment's criticism of the tradition and concerned to affirm traditional belief in a manner consonant with modern perspectives on human existence and its place in the world. In early nineteenth-century Protestant circles, this apologetical approach to the task of faith seeking understanding was known as "mediating theology" (*Vermittlungstheologie*), a designation that took Christian tradition and modern secular culture as the terms to be mediated or reconciled in any modern theological presentation.[3]

Mediating or apologetical theologies, then, frame their task as a dialogue between modern secular culture and Christian tradition. They assume that the interlocutors are enriched by the exchange of perspectives that ensues in the course of the conversation—the Christian tradition by facing the challenge of recent historical, social, and scientific developments within which its own modernity takes shape; secular culture by recognizing that the revisionist commitments of apologetical theologies preclude the reduction of Christian tradition to premodern expressions of its truth-claims. Mediating theologies refuse to regard culture at large as necessarily hostile to the Christian vision or to retreat into the easy security of a narrow confessionalism. Rather they value the mutual understanding that the apologetical conversation can yield and hope that through such a conversation the claims of Christian tradition can gain intelligibility and hence respectability in the modern world.

But the apologetical conversation that a mediating theology conducts can only begin by determining a common ground on which the interlocutors of Christian tradition and secular culture can agree they stand. That common ground can be some form of general human experience, a particular anthropology, or an epistemological or communicative theory. Whatever form it may take, the mediating principle provides an initial point of agreement that might temper or even reconcile the inevitable and often sharp differences between the conversation partners. Moreover, the mediating principle is expected to further the possibility of agreement by posing categories for translating the claims of each dialogue partner to the other. The thought-forms chosen as the mediating principle—whether the philosophies of German idealism or existentialism, a theory of the disclosive power of language, or the worldview of process thought—thus shape the very content of theology as well as facilitate understanding between Christian and secular visions of reality.

One could certainly argue that the search for a common ground for the theological intelligibility of faith, for "foundations" for theological reflection, is as old as theology itself. Yet the explicit, thematic task of constructing a foundational or fundamental theology is a modern enterprise.[4] While the intelligibility of the claims of faith on which theology reflects has been a perennial concern addressed in many ways throughout the entire Christian tradition, the peculiar circumstances of that tradition in the post-Enlightenment world have encouraged theologians to attend to the issue of their discipline's "foundations" in order to justify their portrayal of the gospel message to cultural assumptions, explanations, and practices no longer sympathetic to that message or to premodern procedures for its theological exposition. Foundational or mediating theologies are, then, in their very self-conception, methodologically committed to pleading the case of God's revelation as it has been ecclesially appropriated before the court of modernity. And it is for this reason that so much of what we identify as modern theology is an apologetical, mediating, or foundational enterprise.

Theologians who implicitly by their practice or explicitly by declaration have embraced the nonfoundational perspective have characterized the apologetical approach to theologizing as dysfunctional. In their judgment, post-Enlightenment theology often has corrupted the proper conduct of theology, and so the very

content of Christian doctrine that issues from its skewed interpretations. Typically modern theologies, in their view, form a
tradition of distortion from which authentic contemporary theologies must distinguish themselves and against which authentic
contemporary theologies must remain vigilantly on guard. The
writings of Karl Barth, George Lindbeck, Ronald Thiemann, and
Kathryn Tanner provide interesting illustrations of this diagnosis
and a context for considering nonfoundational solutions to the
modern problematic.

Barth on Liberal Theology

No theologian has influenced our conception of modern theology
more than Karl Barth. His *The Epistle to the Romans* (2d ed.,
1922), one of the few examples of the genre of manifesto in the
history of theology, castigated the liberal Protestant theology of
the previous one hundred years as nothing less than a betrayal
of the Christian gospel in the name of Christianity. For Barth,
theologians since Schleiermacher have been wrongly committed
to satisfying modernity's expectations of proper scientific knowledge, and in their misdirected efforts to please a secular audience
have compromised the integrity of theological interpretation itself. "For me, at any rate," Barth insists in the preface to that work,
"the question of the true nature of interpretation is the supreme
question.—Or is it that these learned men, for whose learning
and erudition I have such genuine respect, fail to recognize the
existence of any real substance at all, of any underlying problem,
of any Word in the words [of theology]?"[5]

In Barth's judgment, theological interpretation in the liberal
tradition of the nineteenth and twentieth centuries has privileged
the human "words" of theological discourse to such a degree
that the revealed Word of God can no longer be distinguished
among them as their subject matter, as the Christian proclamation
to which they are responsible and by which they are judged.
Properly conducted, theology proceeds in full awareness of the
abyss of human sinfulness that separates God and humanity and
that only the graceful revelation of God can bridge. Theology
properly conducted honestly acknowledges its limitations and
knows its work to be the difficult struggle of human words to do
meager justice to the Word of God. The liberal tradition, Barth

argues, is oblivious to these constraints on the theological enterprise, failing even to recognize the distinction—to say nothing of the infinite qualitative distinction—between the Word of God and the words of humanity.

According to *The Epistle to the Romans*, this proclivity to substitute human words for the Word of God is rooted in the fallenness of humanity itself, a fatal consequence of the original sin that permeates history. The most insidious expression of this primal sin is not to be found in hate, violence, or apathy but in religion—for Barth, the human desire to be God. In religion, this most arrogant of aspirations is disguised as piety, morality, and commitment. But the feelings of peace and harmony customarily associated with the religious consciousness only mask the intent of self-deification by which pious fervor for union with the divine is animated. "Religion," Barth declares, "is neither a thing to be enjoyed nor a thing to be celebrated: it must be borne as a yoke which cannot be removed."[6] It is religion that divides humanity and God. Its true reality is "disruption, discord, and the absence of peace."[7] Its only hope for reconciliation lies in the power of grace, by which human sinfulness is both judged and redeemed.

While Barth's portrayal of original sin in *The Epistle to the Romans* is traditional in its description of the inescapability of Adam's fault, its uniqueness lies in its claim that religion, understood as the experience of piety, is actually the clever deceit by which the boundlessness of human arrogance is hidden even from its sinful perpetrator. One should not overlook the extent to which this revision of an age-old doctrine is shaped preeminently by Barth's professed concern in this early writing with the integrity of modern theological interpretation. The typically liberal approach to theologizing from Schleiermacher to Barth's own day regarded piety or religiosity as a universal condition of human experience, and as a mediating principle capable of justifying Christianity's intelligibility to modern culture. One could argue, as Barth does, that this mediating approach to theology is incorrect because it subordinates the Word of God to human words, revelation to experience, and finally the infinite to the finite. But these theological judgments are all the more empowered by the claim of *The Epistle to the Romans* that the experience in which mediating theologies invest their intelligibility is nothing less than an enactment of the primal sin that alienates humanity from God. It is hardly surprising, then, that Barth regards the liberal tradition against which he defined the orientation of his own dialectical theology as itself a promulgation of the history of sin, even as it remains strangely unaware of its actual commitments and motivations.

The conclusion to which this analysis leads is that modern theology is brazenly guilty of celebrating the pretensions of human sinfulness in the very way it posits and builds upon its disciplinary assumptions. The liberal tradition's subjectivist point of departure is, in Barth's estimation, but a theological expression of the exaggerated claims on behalf of human knowledge and achievement that have flourished since the rise of individualism in Western culture. Barth thematizes this historical diagnosis by decrying the "Modernist view" that "goes back to the Renaissance and especially to the Renaissance philosopher Descartes with his proof of God from human self-certainty."[8] "Christian Cartesianism" tries to establish the possibility of an encounter with God's revelation within the natural capacities of humanity, in some mediating principle or foundation on which the possibility of theological knowledge is believed to rest. In this Cartesian style of theologizing, the act of acknowledging the veracity of God's Word "becomes man's own, a predicate of his existence, a content of his consciousness, his possession."[9]

The result of this skewed approach is a "Modernist dogmatics," from beginning to end an anthropology in which the pretense of a theology provides an opportunity for an encomium to all that is human. A Modernist dogmatics "is finally unaware of the fact that in relation to God man has constantly to let something be said to him, has constantly to listen to something, which he constantly does not know and which in no circumstances and in no sense can he say to himself."[10] "Protestant modernism"[11] does not understand theology to be an endeavor undertaken in obedience to grace and in faithfulness to theology's only content offered in the Word of God preached, written, and revealed. Its anthropocentrism, fathomed so clearly Barth believes by the nineteenth-century philosopher Ludwig Feuerbach, may seem to enact the apologetical virtue of widening the Christian proclamation to the farthest reaches of cultural understanding. But finally, for

Barth, the translation of the Christian message that a mediating theology effects is but a clever way in which fallen human nature subverts the revelational content of theology in the name of theology itself.

There can be, Barth maintains, no "foundation, support, or justification" for theology in any philosophy, theory, or epistemology.[12] The foundationalist orientation of theology in the modern age seeks the possibility of knowledge of God *in abstracto* or a priori, presupposing "the existence of a theory of knowledge as a hinterland where the consideration of the truth, worth and competence of the Word of God . . . can for a time at least be suspended."[13] Configured in such a way, theology shirks its disciplinary responsibility. By accepting human knowledge as the criterion for divine revelation, the "Modernist" or "Cartesian" theologian mistakenly concedes that the Word of God stands in need before the claims of noetic expectations, ready to be shaped to the ever-shifting lines of relevance. "God's revelation," Barth asserts, "is a ground which has no higher or deeper ground above or below it but is an absolute ground in itself, and therefore for man a court from which there can be no possible appeal to a higher court." And precisely because revelation has "its reality and truth wholly and in every respect . . . within itself,"[14] the dogmatic task of expounding its promise in faith and for the church proceeds properly only by respecting the integrity of its proclamation.

In Barth's critique, the typically apologetical style of modern theology seems to constitute a "tradition" of natural theology, which Barth defines as "the doctrine of a union of man with God existing outside God's revelation in Jesus Christ."[15] That spurious union may seem to occur in any dimension of the cultural world, from the depths of subjectivity to the deeds that shape the public realm. But in the disciplinary structure of theology its vain claims appear as the mediating principle or "foundation" on which apologetical theologies ground their enterprise of justifying and translating the gospel to modern culture at large. While natural theology has usually been understood in the history of Christian thought as *metaphysical* speculation intent on knowing God through the world, Barth reconceives this rationalist project in *The Epistle to the Romans* and in the early volumes of *Church*

Dogmatics as the priority of *methodological* construction in theology, and so as a peculiarly modern preoccupation with a century-long history of its own.

There is no evidence that nonfoundational philosophy influenced Barth's critique of modern theology in any way, or that he was even familiar with the small body of philosophical work advocating the nonfoundational perspective that had appeared by the early decades of the twentieth century. Nevertheless, Barth's characterization of modern theology suggests interesting parallels to the portrait of modern metaphysics offered by the pragmatists at the turn of the century. Like the nonfoundational philosophers, Barth presents his own position as a cure for a disciplinary malady diagnosed as the pretentious search for immediate and certain truth in some dimension of human subjectivity. Like the nonfoundational philosophers, Barth understands the modern preoccupation with methodological first principles as a formal way of making exaggerated claims for the capacities of human knowledge. And like the nonfoundational philosophers, Barth objectifies these errors as particularly modern, as part and parcel of a corrupt epistemic tradition worthy only of rejection.

This last point calls our attention to the degree to which Barth's powerful influence on twentieth-century theology has been instrumental in defining the very rubric of "modern theology" not only as a historical periodization but also as a pejorative designation for the theological task from the perspective of nonfoundational values. One also finds this negative characterization of modern theology in the explicitly nonfoundational theologies of George Lindbeck, Ronald Thiemann, and Kathryn Tanner.

Lindbeck on Doctrine

George Lindbeck's call for a nonfoundational approach to theology in his influential book *The Nature of Doctrine* (1984) addresses what he judges to be the unhappy fate of Christianity in the modern age. Lindbeck is convinced that the ethos, values, and directions of modernity have subsumed those of the Christian tradition and through that subsumption Christianity in the modern world is threatened with the loss of its identity. Lindbeck understands the modern or liberal tradition that has had such deleterious effects on Christianity to extend from the age of the

Enlightenment to the present. Only now, at this juncture in its history, can the church fully recognize the consequences of modernity for its belief and practice, and mark a critical position from which to distinguish its own agenda from that of modernity. For Lindbeck, the advent of this postliberal age, at least from a Christian perspective, provides the church with an opportunity for naming and strengthening its identity amid the culture of pluralism.

Distinguishing among premodern, modern or liberal, and postliberal conceptualizations of doctrine elucidates for Lindbeck the changing understandings of Christian normativeness that highlight the plight of Christian integrity in modern culture. Preponderantly in premodern times but also in the present, doctrines have been understood as propositions, as sentences whose truthfulness is established by their abiding correspondence to ontological realities. This cognitivist approach to doctrine has become problematic in the modern age because of its difficulty in accounting for the fact of doctrinal development recognized since the rise of historical consciousness. In modern or post-Enlightenment times, doctrines commonly have been understood as "noninformative and nondiscursive symbols of inner feelings, attitudes, or existential orientations."[16] This "experiential-expressivist" conception of doctrine, Lindbeck claims, invests the corporate inner life of believers with veridical authority and sees doctrinal expression as language's qualified and ever-revisable efforts to articulate experiential truth.

Experiential-expressivism is able to account for the development of doctrine by portraying ecclesial teaching as a function of the historicity of experience, and largely for this reason it has won the favor of modernity as the preferred conceptualization of Christian truth-claims. But the difficulty Lindbeck finds with this approach is that its subjectivist orientation seems willing in principle to relinquish the abiding normativeness of Christian tradition, so clearly affirmed in a propositionalist view of doctrine, for the sake of a coherent explanation of doctrine's historicity. Like philosophers critical of Cartesian claims for the authority of immediate experience, Lindbeck argues that the experiential foundation of the modern conception of doctrine cannot bear the burden of Christian coherence, consistency, and identity, especially in an age whose values are antithetical to those of the tradition. Indeed, for Lindbeck, the experiential-expressivist conception of doctrine is a product of modernity's at the very least dubious influence on Christianity.

Since the time of Schleiermacher, Christian believers in general and theologians in particular have found the experiential-expressive understanding of doctrine to be compatible with the "psychosocial" matrix of modernity. In an age in which religiosity often is equated with "individual quests for personal meaning," symbolic views of doctrine both privilege the authority of individual experience and relativize doctrine's ecclesial value as the expression of a common faith. Such a regard for doctrine proceeds from the assumption that religions are "multiple suppliers of different forms of a single commodity needed for transcendent self-expression and self-realization."[17] The marketability of religiosity in this experiential-expressivist model is, for Lindbeck, one important source of its appeal. Another is the suitability of its categories for reaching virtually unqualified agreement in interdenominational and even interreligious dialogue. If all religious experience is fundamentally the same, then the religions of the world are expressions of a single subjective truth to which any individual has immediate access. While this view might foster mutual respect among religions, its final consequence for all of them might very well be the fate that Lindbeck fears for Christianity under the experiential-expressivist model: the loss of religious particularity and so of the distinctiveness of ecclesial community as the church increasingly becomes indistinguishable from the culture at large.

As communal traditions are commended only as "optional aids in individual self-realization rather than as bearers of normative realities to be interiorized,"[18] their capacity to withstand the psychological and social currents of modernity increasingly diminishes. Lindbeck does not look nostalgically to premodern assumptions and configurations of doctrine as a panacea for the difficulties of Christianity in the modern world. Nor does he anticipate a reconciliation between Christianity and modern culture cast in terms defined by the former instead of the latter. The power of modernity could be countered at least within the church,

Lindbeck believes, by a postliberal or "cultural-linguistic" understanding of doctrine, one in which doctrines are conceived to function "not as expressive symbols or as truth claims, but as communally authoritative rules of discourse, attitude, and action."[19] From this perspective, Christian doctrines are not merely derivative of the inner life but constitute an objective network of beliefs to which experience owes any coherence that it might possess. Like cultures or languages, doctrines function in this conceptualization as a normative idiom or grammar measuring skills and governing the meaningful practices of religious believers. And like the rules that implicitly or explicitly regulate cultures and languages, doctrines in a cultural-linguistic conceptualization provide stable and yet flexible, developing guidelines for the formation of Christian identity among modernity's competing claims, values, and practices.

While Lindbeck offers his diagnosis of modernity's foundationalist proclivities from a sociological viewpoint, Ronald Thiemann and Kathryn Tanner reach much the same conclusions from a doctrinal perspective.

Thiemann and Tanner on Theological Priorities

In his *Revelation and Theology* (1985), Thiemann argues for the need for a nonfoundational theology in the face of modernity's corruption of the traditional doctrine of revelation. The pressures upon Christianity from the Enlightenment, he believes, have resulted not merely in an adjustment of that doctrine's classical claims and mode of expression but in a striking and deleterious modification of its content. The sixteenth-century Protestant reformers made the doctrine of divine prevenience utterly central to any theological consideration of human knowledge of God. In their view, the Christian message of salvation is the proclamation of the grace of God, but a proclamation that understands the priority of grace to everything human and the reliance of every human experience, word, and act on the power of divine grace. Thiemann is convinced, however, that "in modern doctrines of revelation the reformers' basic conviction regarding the prevenience of God's grace no longer functions as a background belief,"[20] as an indispensable affirmation of ecclesial faithfulness. Modern theological treatments of the doctrine of revelation have vitiated the doctrine of prevenience in their readiness to placate the epistemic expectations of post-Enlightenment intellectual culture.

Modern doctrines of revelation, Thiemann charges, become at least in part "theoretical justifications for the Christian claim to knowledge of God."[21] Lacking confidence in the explanatory sufficiency of prevenience for a cogent modern treatment of revelation, post-Enlightenment theologians have turned to foundationalist argumentation in order to justify Christian belief to a contemporary audience. Theological foundationalism may appear in any number of argumentative forms, but all embrace the premise that the integrity of human claims for knowledge of God cannot simply be justified within the circle of belief, but must be demonstrated by rational inference grounded finally on some common intuition experientially available to all. For Thiemann, this Cartesian approach wrongly makes the immediacy of human subjectivity a first principle of coherence for theological reflection. To the degree that the foundationalist enterprise becomes key to human claims for the knowledge of God, "modern doctrines of revelation inevitably become epistemological doctrines."[22]

The priority of epistemology in modern approaches to theology could be countered, Thiemann thinks, by acknowledging the proper role of reasoning in the theological task. Faithfulness to Christianity's basic background beliefs, and not their theoretical justification, measures the responsibility of theological reasoning. This confusion of priorities has had disastrous consequences for the issue of knowledge of God in modernity, as faithlessness to the doctrine of the prevenience of God's grace has led to the desire on the part of "most theologians . . . to discard the doctrine of revelation."[23] While one might find this judgment to be somewhat overstated, it does express Thiemann's view that the problem lies not in this or that misguided theological effort but in the character of modern theology as such. For Thiemann, the implication of modern theology's epistemological priorities is that its disciplinary commitments have become Pelagian or semi-Pelagian at best. This implied, doctrinal heuristic in Thiemann's analysis is made explicit by Kathryn Tanner in her book *God and Creation in Christian Theology* (1988).

Distinguishing in broad terms between the theological sensibilities of "ancients" and "moderns," Tanner diagnoses the contemporary problem faced by Christian communities as the "modern breakdown of theological discourse."[24] The doctrine of the
God-world relationship, rather than the doctrine of revelation,
serves as her test case. Invoking Lindbeck's cultural-linguistic
model, Tanner argues that authentic Christian discourse over the
centuries has produced rules for articulating God's relationship
to creatures. The tradition commends Christians to "avoid both
a simple univocal attribution of predicates to God and world and
a simple contrast of divine and nondivine predicates," a norm
for Christian discourse that might be called the rule of transcen-
dence and immanence. At the same time, the tradition expects
competent speakers of the Christian language to "avoid in talk
about God's creative agency all suggestions of limitation in scope
or manner,"[25] a norm that might be called the rule of the utter
efficacy of grace.

Modern theological discourse, Tanner argues, has relinquished
responsibility particularly to the second, and so indirectly to the
first, of these rules. By allowing the spurious ascendancy of a
priori methods and anthropologies of human self-sufficiency
within their discipline, modern revisionist theologians have vitiated both the logic and the content of traditional Christian discourse. In fact, the consequences of revisionist construction have
been so pervasive and consistent that even discourse concerning
a doctrine as basic as the God-world relationship has been corrupted by a language similar in vocabulary to, but utterly different
in grammatical structure from, the teachings of the Christian
tradition.

For Tanner, the upshot of this foundationalist approach is that
"Pelagianism of some sort becomes arguably the dominant motif
in modern theology."[26] Like this ancient heresy, modern theology
privileges human capacities in representing the relationship between God and creatures. The result, Tanner suggests, is that
modern theology departs from the communally authoritative
rules for its proper conduct, appealing instead to an illegitimate
grounding for its enterprise in an understanding of human nature
at odds with Christianity's most central beliefs on the priority of
grace and the fallenness of humanity. In other words, theological

foundationalism is at least one modern and methodological expression of ancient Pelagianism. Faced with this inconsistency in the procedure and content of theology, "the theologian must block the Pelagian implications that modern claims about the world and humans will suggest in talk about the creature's own capacities."[27] Tanner urges theologians to be untypically modern by cultivating the traditional meaning of theological language in an age in which it has been all but lost.

The respective characterizations of modernity in the work of Lindbeck, Thiemann, and Tanner as a period of privileged subjectivity, foundationalist reasoning, and fractured theological discourse follow in the steps of Barth's earlier effort to portray modernity as an age theologically at odds with traditional Christian faith. Central to the work of Lindbeck, Thiemann, and Tanner, however, is an explicit appeal to the critique of foundationalism as an invaluable aid in diagnosing the malady of modern theology. This critique, suggested but not developed thematically in Barth's analysis, is especially adept in exposing the misplaced allegiances of modern theology's own assumptions and so of the logical inferences that proceed from them. Yet the nonfoundational perspective they commend offers more than a diagnosis of theological modernity. It also suggests ways in which modern theologians can be faithful to traditional Christian claims by adopting a modestly constructive approach to their discipline in line with the nonfoundational critique. It is to examples of this theological program that we now turn.

Against Theory: Theology as Nonfoundational Description

Were we to seek the object of the nonfoundational theologian's critical disdain we would need to look no further than the theories to which foundational theologies have appealed in order to justify their intelligibility. Our discussion of Quine and Sellars in the previous chapter examined the difficulties faced by traditional understandings of theorizing under the nonfoundational critique. The customary view of theories as complete, fully interpreted, and universal explanations becomes questionable from the nonfoundational perspective, as does the notion of philosophy itself as a disciplinary exercise in theorizing.

As consequential as that critique has proved to be for traditional understandings of the philosophical task, it has not at all necessarily ended in despair about the possibility of knowledge and the philosophical task as such. Quine's radical empiricism, for example, criticizes customary views of knowledge but outlines a holistic understanding of its proper constitution. Rorty rejects the project of traditional philosophy as a search for the foundations of knowledge but hopes that a critical hermeneutics will fill the cultural space created by the demise of epistemology. Similar revisionist results ensue as the nonfoundational critique is applied in a theological setting. Suspicions of the role played by theory in mediating theologies do not lead nonfoundational theologians to despair about the possibility of a modern theology. As misguided and detrimental as they believe foundational theologies to be, nonfoundational theologians are reform-minded and committed to setting guidelines for theological reflection that respect both the limitations of human knowing and the context in which they believe theological reasoning meaningfully to flourish. The concrete proposals of George Lindbeck and Ronald Thiemann may serve as illustrations.

Postliberal Intratextuality

The cultural-linguistic model of doctrine Lindbeck proposes in *The Nature of Doctrine* serves a theological program that he describes as "nonfoundational" or "postliberal." If it is the holistic world of Christian doctrine and practice that poses a meaningful frame of reference for the believer's experience rather than the opposite, then the consequences of this perspective for theology are striking. Theology, configured in terms of such a view of normativeness, would need to accord interpretive priority to the authority of the doctrinal tradition, to the rules for the right understanding of scripture that have emerged from its reading in the ecclesial community through the ages.

Modern theologies typically measure their interpretive faithfulness in a twofold manner, in terms of their adequacy both to the scriptural text and to contemporary experience. Such theologies are confident that the judicious correlation of text and experience will disclose the mutual relations between the truth

of Christian revelation and the truth of human experience. Lindbeck fears that this view of faithfulness is inescapably foundationalist. Correlational interpretation, he argues, does not recognize the priority of the normative, "ruled" meaning of scripture
within the church's doctrinal tradition. Instead, the correlational
approach widens the scope of interpretive normativeness so
much that the ecclesial context of theological understanding loses
all specificity. A correlational theology in principle favors the
experiential pole of theology. And so privileged, contemporary
experience can readily be configured as both a foundational
theory of interpretation and as the interpreted content of
theology itself.

A nonfoundational or postliberal theology, Lindbeck asserts,
would understand theological faithfulness as intratextuality.
Above all, this term refers to the theologian's exclusive commitment to the authority of the biblical text and its validated understanding in the doctrinal tradition for any theological decision,
judgment, or interpretation. Intratextual faithfulness eschews a
correlational understanding of theological responsibility. In consonance with a cultural-linguistic view of doctrine, a postliberal
theology holds that "it is the religion instantiated in Scripture
which defines being, truth, goodness, and beauty, and [that] the
nonscriptural exemplifications of these realities need to be trans-
formed into figures (or types or antitypes) of the scriptural ones."
In a notable statement that condemns the correlational method
by reversing the usual lines of theological interpretation, Lindbeck
claims that "it is the text, so to speak, which absorbs the world,
rather than the world the text."[28] It is less difficult to understand
that Christianity's authoritative textual tradition functions as a
meaningful framework or "semiotic system" for believers than
that the same textual tradition has the capacity to absorb a world
that often names its values without appeal, even by way of opposition, to Christianity. Yet Lindbeck attributes such power to
the biblical story and measures its strength not by any extraneous
criterion but by the lives of Christians throughout the centuries
who were and continue to be utterly compelled by its message
of salvation.

The text's capacity to absorb the world is first of all a practice
that unfolds in faithful acts of theological description. "Intratextual

theology," Lindbeck proposes, "redescribes reality within the scriptural framework rather than translating Scripture into extrascriptural categories."[29] The cultural anthropologist Clifford Geertz's understanding of the ethnographer's work as "thick description" provides Lindbeck with an analogy for the theologian's craft. Like the anthropologist, the theologian is not well served by interpretive theories imported from outside a culture, nor by generalizations from within that same culture that all too quickly become pristine abstractions divorced from the very realities they purport to explain. Ever resisting reason's penchant for speculation, the theologian must offer a close, detailed description of scriptural meaning and the many ways the circumstances of individuals, societies, and histories can find coherence, wisdom, and fulfillment within its narrative world.

Such theological description needs to be "literally intratextual,"[30] but this literality does not obviate the role of creativity in the theological enterprise. "There is, indeed," Lindbeck claims, "no more demanding exercise of the imaginative and inventive powers than to explore how a language, culture, or religion may be employed to give meaning to new domains of thought, reality, and action."[31] When theological description is truly creative it shows how the text's absorption of the world can actually be accomplished in Christian practice. The presence of the text in the lives of believers as a medium for ordering their experience, words, and deeds is the real measure of theological analysis. This narrative understanding of the Christian life suggests an ecclesiology in which participation in the church is determined by the believer's commitment to its intratextual reality. As foreign as this view of the church may be to the contemporary climate, its practical advantage over typically liberal construals of the place of the church in the modern world lies in its recognition that ecclesial relevance is meaningless without an ecclesial identity to foster.

Interpretive faithfulness as intratextuality has methodological implications that bring us directly to Lindbeck's commendation for a nonfoundational approach to theology. Modern theology has especially been committed to the apologetic enterprise, undertaken in the theological subdiscipline of fundamental or foundational theology, as a way of validating the intelligibility of Christian claims before the epistemic demands of post-Enlightenment culture. Lindbeck recognizes that the liberal concern for the intellectual credibility of the faith is shaped by its hopes for dialogue with the modern world. These hopes appear in the very method of foundational theology, specifically in the "foundational enterprise of uncovering universal principles or structures—if not metaphysical, then existential, phenomenological, or hermeneutical."[32] Apologetical theologies appeal to such universal theories as "foundations" for theological knowledge, as a neutral ground, so to speak, on which Christianity might meet the testy conversation partner of modernity, as first principles both acceptable to modernity and able to convey the intelligibility of Christian claims. But the nonfoundational critique of knowledge advanced by philosophers concludes that there are no universals and that theorizing is incapable of the grand act of translation liberal theologians seem to expect of the apologetical endeavor.

"Postliberals," Lindbeck states, "are bound to be skeptical . . . about apologetics and foundations."[33] The indefensibility of foundationalist logic is one reason for this skepticism, but Lindbeck's doubts about foundational theologies seem to stem more from sociological concerns than from judgments about right philosophy. The liberal devotion to foundational theory, however logically questionable, finally matters little if the preeminent challenge for the church is the cultivation of its own language and practice in an age in which "Christendom is passing and Christians are becoming a diaspora."[34] Lindbeck acknowledges that the postliberal approach will not be attractive to those concerned with the church from a statistical perspective, with membership figures, church attendance, and the influence the church gains from having larger numbers of its adherents at work in society at large. But church membership and its influence are of small concern if the church has no particular claims of its own to hold and to profess. The foundational approach to theology contributes to the loss of Christian particularity because it measures the intelligibility of the gospel message by criteria set for it by the culture at large. That culture's radical pluralism actually enters the method of theology in the various foundational theories employed as media for translating the gospel to the world. And, unsurprisingly, that same pluralism permeates the results of that translation as extrabiblical categories, content, and meaning are systematically substituted for the doctrinally ruled scriptural narration that Christians have traditionally taken to be normative.

Lindbeck's suspicion of theory, however, is not a consequence of a fideistic retreat from the powers of reason and the role they play in theological interpretation. "Antifoundationalism," he assures his reader, "is not to be equated with irrationalism." Even if there are universal canons of rationality to which theology, like all intellectual constructs, is responsible, it is unlikely that these canons, and the operations of reasoning itself, could be "formulated in some neutral, framework-independent language."[35] Rationality as it actually functions is context-specific. If this is so, the intelligibility of intellectual constructs—from scientific theory, to hermeneutics, to theological interpretation itself—must be measured in terms that are context-specific. From the perspective of Lindbeck's postliberalism, that context is the ecclesial culture that believes and lives by the language of God's story.

Within the meaningful framework of ecclesial life, intelligibility is a matter of "skill, not theory, and credibility comes from good performance, not adherence to independently formulated criteria."[36] Theological skill, much more the product of arduously practiced craftsmanship than native genius, is a talent for applying the rules of the doctrinal tradition to the ever-changing circumstances of life, culture, and history. To use Lindbeck's well-known phrase again, it is skill in showing the text's capacity to absorb the world. This skill is not put to the service of an imaginative translation, in thrall to a theoretical explanation accounting in the end for both culture *and* the gospel. Rather it is a skill applied ad hoc, one that meets the contingencies of time, space, and circumstance as they arise, and uses whatever means are helpful for describing their intratextual significance.[37]

While Lindbeck portrays this configuration of the theological task as a "highly constructive enterprise," he is careful to distinguish postliberal from liberal theological construction. A descriptive, nonfoundational theology "resembles ancient catechesis more than modern translation."[38] Its constructive work lies in the detailed description of the biblical text, an interpretive approach that has become as necessary as the content of that text has become foreign to both culture and the church. Unlike the correlational style of construction that so many modern theologians

have quickly made their own, the descriptive construction that
Lindbeck commends is finally instruction in which insightfulness
is valued in the context of good ecclesial pedagogy, and relevance
judged by the standard of scriptural priority and particularity.

Ad Hoc Reasoning

The nonfoundational criticism to which Lindbeck alludes in his
argument becomes explicit in Ronald Thiemann's spirited defense
of the traditional doctrine of revelation. Rational justification is a
task incumbent on anyone seeking the logical integrity of their
intellectual claims, including theologians. But rational justification, Thiemann points out, is an ad hoc procedure, since the
sufficient reasons offered for one's beliefs "will vary from case
to case, depending on the difficulty of the belief and the person
or persons to be convinced."[39] This contingency in the procedure
of justifying belief stems from the character of human knowledge
itself. Knowledge, including theological knowledge, is not be-
holden to a universal standard or norm for determining its truth
or even its cogency. Rather, rational justification takes place within
a specific community of knowers. And that community is a complex, epistemic network of ever-shifting arguments, circumstances, audiences, criteria for justification, and even understandings
of what rationality is and how it goes about its business. Rational
justification, then, is context-specific and pragmatic in its operation. "In practice," Thiemann claims, "we define sufficient reason
to be reason enough to convince the relevant party."[40]

The modern or, in Thiemann's judgment, foundational mode
of theological argumentation founders on the mistaken assumption that rational justification needs more than pragmatic consensus to establish its validity. Knowledge, for the foundationalist,
requires final grounds:

> Proponents of such [epistemological] doctrines fear that unless
> some *ultimately* sufficient reason is discovered, then all other
> reasons will be groundless and without foundation. Appeals to
> "reason enough" will be arbitrary unless some final Sufficient
> Reason is discerned. Reasons may ordinarily depend on other
> reasons for their support, but the entire network of interrelated
> reasons will be without justification unless grounded in an ultimate
> reason.[41]

An "ultimate reason," of course, cannot be a mere abstraction. So once the need for a ground for knowledge becomes entrenched in epistemic expectations, the foundationalist's task involves the determination of such a ground. It entails the actual discovery of a "self-evident, noninferential belief"[42] establishing the theoretical possibility of the very endeavor of justifying belief. The "foundation" for knowledge usually takes the form of an immediate intuition outside the chain of rational justification. Without such a noninferential basis, the foundationalist fears, the inferences linked together in the chain of rational justification will regress infinitely, finally presenting a circular argument for what they intend to explain and so no argument at all.

Modern theology's own "Cartesian anxiety" surfaces in the effort to establish a theoretical underpinning for knowledge of God in a noninferential experience, the subjective product of some natural capacity intelligible to those both in and outside the church and serving to justify the possibility of theological inference. It is precisely this theological version of foundationalism that violates the classical Christian belief in God's prevenience.

Invoking Richard Rorty's thesis in *Philosophy and the Mirror of Nature*, Thiemann argues that the "modern epistemological defense of God's prevenience fails because it confuses *rational justification* and *causal explanation*."[43] Foundational theologies equate these exercises, as though convincing theological argumentation required first principles whose causal authority was evident throughout their inferential effects. This reduction of rational justification to causal explanation stems from the apologist's desire to identify an experience outside the web of Christian belief that both establishes the integrity of that belief *and* satisfies the noetic demands of intellectual culture. Oddly enough, Thiemann points out, that causal principle cannot be the divine revelation to which Christians through the ages have appealed in faith and through grace as the content of theological justification. God's revelation is by no means epistemologically neutral and so unable to serve as a causal explanation for theological claims satisfactory to those outside the circle of faith. The foundational appeal to an intuitive discernment moored in human subjectivity may offer the possibility of an apologetical theology vaguely intelligible to those outside the church. But it does so at the cost of the traditional belief of the church that the knowledge of God is itself the work of God and not the product of any human act. The epistemological Pelagianism of modernity can be corrected, Thiemann believes, by a nonfoundational theology. Like Lindbeck, Thiemann understands such an approach to be marked by its opposition to the theoretical first principles of apologetical theologies and committed to the traditional doctrine of God's prevenience in the very method of theological interpretation.[44]

A nonfoundational theology would regard the enterprise of faith seeking understanding "as primarily a descriptive activity, a second-order mode of reflection which displays the logic inherent in Christian belief and practice."[45] In other words, a nonfoundational theology would recognize the contextuality of its endeavor. Like any interpretive activity, theological description involves the justification of belief. Unlike foundational theologies, however, this approach does not make the task of justifying belief responsible to an extra-ecclesial audience. "Nonfoundational justification," Thiemann claims, "requires the assumption that there is a Christian conceptual frame supported by specific conventions and practices," and that these are defined by "the Christian faith, community, and tradition."[46] In such a contextualized approach to the theological task, the foundationalist proclivity for theorizing becomes superfluous. Since it finds no need to justify belief to an intellectual culture at large, a descriptive theology does not seek a universal principle of translation and so can dispense with a method that is not only detrimental to Christian belief but also logically suspect.

With direct reference to the understanding of justification espoused by Quine, Thiemann portrays descriptive theology as "holist justification," "a process of rational persuasion" that "consists . . . in seeking the relation between a disputed belief and the web of interrelated beliefs within which it rests."[47] One of the most basic beliefs within that network is the Christian claim that God's reality, power, and salvational efficacy are prior to, and the source of, all creaturely reality, power, and initiative. This belief in God's prevenience, Thiemann notes, is disclosed in the language and the logic of the scriptural narrative, which presents the gospel's salvational message as the promise that God *already* has acted on behalf of sinful humanity. Holistic justification sets its task as the faithful description of that divine promise for the life of the church.

A nonfoundational approach to theology provides no guarantee of interpretive success. In the end, the church's practice of God's narrated promise measures the adequacy of any ad hoc theological interpretation. Thiemann, however, believes that the superiority of nonfoundational to foundational theologies lies in their methodological consistency with that narrated promise and its supposition of the utter prevenience of grace. By insisting that the scriptural narrative sets the meaningful framework for Christian practice, including the Christian practice that it itself is, a nonfoundational theology acknowledges the graceful activity of God by which the ecclesial community believes itself to be shaped, and so the divine initiative by which the theological interpretation of that community is also properly shaped and to which it is solely responsible. Unlike the self-contradictory enterprise that Thiemann believes foundational theology to be, descriptive theology affirms the consistency between theological content and method. For Thiemann as for Lindbeck, method is not ancillary to the Christian faith that theology expounds, but a *locus* among the claims that the church counts as central to belief. Theological interpretation is not primarily the endeavor of individual imagination, but an act proceeding from and faithful to the church. Like the holistic justification it offers, theological interpretation is thoroughly enmeshed in the motivation, commitment, and faith of the tradition.

Narrative Realism, the Particularity of Jesus, and Christian Practice

Hans Frei (1922–1988) would agree wholeheartedly that theological interpretation should understand itself as a Christian act. Theological reflection, he claims, is "for the believer, a pleasurable exercise in arranging or, as I should prefer to say, ordering his thinking about his faith and—in a certain sense—a praise of God by the use of the analytical capacities."[48] While one could find similar descriptions of the theological enterprise in any age, there is something about Frei's doxological understanding of the priorities of theology in the modern period that makes it most compatible with the nonfoundational perspective. In his published work, Hans Frei does not identify his approach as nonfoundational. Yet Frei's contribution to the theological formulation of that position has been profound. Indeed, it would not be an exaggeration to say that Frei has had the single greatest influence on the development of the nonfoundational perspective in the field of theology. This influence can be seen in the way that self-professed nonfoundational thinkers like Lindbeck and Thiemann have relied on Frei's ideas. More importantly, though, Frei's work itself offers an insightful diagnosis of theological modernity and suggests what, in light of the label offered by others, can be described as a nonfoundational alternative to typically modern configurations of scriptural authority, especially the normative status of scripture's portrayal of Jesus Christ for theology.

Biblical Narrative

Frei assesses the problem of scriptural authority in modern theology in the thesis of his important book *The Eclipse of Biblical Narrative* (1974). Prior to the appearance of historical-critical readings of scripture in the eighteenth century, Frei argues, the biblical text had been read realistically, that is, as literal accounts of reality. "The words and sentences meant what they said, and because they did so they accurately described real events and real truths that were rightly put only in those terms and no others."[49] Literal readings, which assumed a realistic regard for the scriptural narrative, and figural readings, which extended this realism to the biblical canon as a unitary whole, were self-referential in a certain sense. They pointed the reader to the Bible's narrative world as God's story about her or his life and invited the reader to accept this world as the proper setting for understanding that life and the lives of others. With the advent of historical criticism, however, the realistic reading of scripture began to break down or, to invoke the metaphor Frei chose for the title of his book, to be eclipsed by another type of reading foreign to the way in which scripture had always been read.

Realistic narrative, Frei claims, "is that kind in which subject and social setting belong together, and characters and external circumstances fitly render each other." Subject matter and depiction are one in realistic narrative. "Neither character nor circumstance separately, nor yet their interaction, is a shadow of something else more real or more significant. Nor is the one," Frei adds, "more important than the other in the story."[50] While moderns have come to know this genre through certain kinds of fictional writing, particularly realistic novels, premodern sensibilities took for granted that the Bible offered the reader a realistic portrait of God's relations with humanity, a sacred plot determined by the complex nexus of character and circumstance. Like the other nonfoundational theologians we have considered, Frei believes that the advent of modernity has had dire consequences for traditional Christian understanding, and he traces their cause to the loss of a realistic reading of the Bible and so to the loss of scripture's own narrative sense.

By the eighteenth century and through the interpretive venue of historical criticism, scriptural commentators began to regard the realistic character of the biblical narrative as unimportant or even superfluous. "It is fascinating," Frei observes,

> that the realistic character of the crucial biblical stories was actually acknowledged and agreed upon by most of the significant eighteenth-century commentators. But since the precritical analytical or interpretive procedure for isolating it had irretrievably broken down in the opinion of most commentators, this specifically realistic characteristic, though acknowledged by all hands to be there, finally came to be ignored, or—even more fascinating—its presence or distinctiveness came to be denied for lack of a "method" to isolate it.[51]

The realistic trait of scripture, after all, did not require a theory or method for its elucidation, but only the appreciation of the faithful interpreter. In the eyes of precritical believers, the narrative character of scripture was so inseparable from its meaning that the description of its literal sense was taken to be the proper interpretive approach. Descriptive accession to the authority of the literal sense—so edifying, consoling, and finally saving to the believer prior to the dawn of modernity—proved to be unsatisfying to historical-critical interpreters. In their reading, the precritical unity of scripture's realistic quality and its meaning was divided by the expectation that scripture's meaning could not be equated with its realistic or "history-like" account, since critical reasoning had demonstrated convincingly that the events of the narrative certainly could not have occurred as described. Historical-critical interpretation posed its own standard of the text's intelligibility in which "explicative meaning was reference."[52] Even those modern interpreters who held that the Bible did not mean what it said were inclined, and usually eager, to affirm that the Bible had a meaning to express. But that meaning, the Bible's real subject matter they assumed, lay outside the words of the text and could be fathomed only by taking the text as a reference to it. Whether they took reference to be to an idea, a historically reconstructed and so credible core of the history-like narrative, or a doctrine, the modern interpreters of the Bible— rationalists, speculative philosophers, and eventually even confessing theologians—accepted the unbiblical framework of a general hermeneutics for the explication of textual meaning, and in doing so abandoned the traditional conception of the Bible's narrative realism.

If nonfoundational criticism involves the identification of spurious epistemic positions falsely privileged within knowledge's holistic weaving of contextual claims, then Frei's thesis in *The Eclipse of Biblical Narrative* might very well be seen as a nonfoundational assessment of modern biblical interpretation. For Frei, the narrative or realistic character of the Bible is an indispensable dimension of scriptural authority. The Bible's realistic or history-like depiction of its claims affirms the integrity of those same claims by insisting that *these* words, *these* events, and *these* lives present the story of God's salvation of humanity. Historical-critical exegesis reduced scripture's narrative sense to unimportant matters of historical fact or to the exaggerated imaginings of religious myth, thus vitiating the very context for the Bible's meaning. The biblical hermeneutics which followed in the steps of historical criticism defined its task as the delineation of a method or theory to facilitate the act of reference beyond the scriptural narrative, where the new apologetics located the Bible's real meaning. This extrabiblical referent—whether it was envisioned as moral virtue, the religious self-consciousness, or the fulfillment of history—and the theory for its elucidation served as something of a foundation upon which the results of exegesis finally depended for their intelligibility.

The Character of Jesus

Frei's thesis has interesting implications for theological interpretation, specifically in the area of christology. In a Christian reading of the Bible, after all, it is the person of Jesus Christ to whom the narrative refers, both in its parts and as a whole. Meaning-as-reference may satisfy the apologetical search for a foundational truth outside the terms set by scripture for its own understanding. The consequences of that search, however, are more than exegetical. The referential approach to biblical hermeneutics finally assumes that Jesus means something other than himself, a view that repudiates the church's confession of who Jesus is and so too its most basic claims about what being a follower of Jesus entails. In light of this mutual relationship between narrative sense and christology, it is hardly surprising that while he was writing *The Eclipse of Biblical Narrative* Frei was fine-tuning a theological experiment entitled *The Identity of Jesus Christ* (1975). Each project undoubtedly informed the other.

This short work, which might be described as a meditation on the reality of grace, explores the believer's encounter with Jesus Christ, and does so by demonstrating at the same time an approach to theological interpretation consistent with its subject matter. Modern expositions of Christ's identity, Frei argues, have mistakenly assumed that experiences of his presence, and particularly explanations of "*how* Christ is present to us and *how* we can believe in his presence," provide the only intelligible answers to the formal question of who Christ is.[53] These explanations of the possibility of Christ's presence for belief appeal to criteria or reasons outside the biblical narrative and thus serve as theoretical justifications that are unnecessary for, and moreover distort, the encounter with Jesus Christ in faith. "Needless to say, when the term 'presence' has become just a question of theory, it no longer has any use in describing the relation between Christ and believers."[54] Identity and presence are entirely one in Christ, Frei claims, and their unity must be reflected in theological analysis. But even though identity and presence are given to us together in Christ, it behooves us to speak of Christ's presence in light of claims about who he is. "Talk about Christ's identity and presence," Frei proposes, "should be in that order, rather than the reverse, even though identity and presence are one in him as he relates himself to us."[55]

Establishing the priority of the identity of Christ is important to Frei for several reasons. First, the foundational role accorded to experience in imaginative speculations about the "how" of Christ's presence can be checked by highlighting the centrality of "who" Jesus is. Frei examines a number of extrabiblical portraits of Christ figures, from gnostic myths to the modern literary sketches of Herman Melville, Nikos Kazantzakis, and Graham Greene, to demonstrate that the priority of Christ's presence to his identity in these works unfailingly leads to the distortion of the Jesus of the New Testament, as his story is made to refer to another. Second, insisting on the priority of Jesus' identity turns the believer to the only place his character is displayed, that is, in the realistic portraits of Matthew, Mark, Luke, and John. The biblical narrative requires no method for the elucidation of its meaning. Its realism offers the only context for its meaning that in turn can be appreciated through what we might call an insightful reiteration by the theological interpreter. Frei is confident that such a faithful description of the Jesus of the Gospels will yield both an authentic depiction of his identity and, in that identity, a trustworthy guide for considerations of his presence to the believer.

The identity of any person, Frei observes, "is the self-referral, or ascription to him, of his physical and personal states, properties, characteristics, and actions."[56] Frei resists the modern penchant toward psychologizing or spiritualizing personal identity. A person's identity, he proposes, can better be approached through descriptions of his or her enacted intentions, and in the way those enacted intentions manifest the continuity in change that a person's life is. An appreciative description of the Gospels shows Jesus' identity to be enacted in his obedience to God's will, in the transition from power to powerlessness in the course of his life as he accepts and endures his passion and death, and in his willingness to embrace God's plan for the salvation of humanity through his resurrection from the dead. For Frei, "God's deed in raising Jesus is actually a deed in which the identity of

Jesus is *manifested*, rather than being the achievement of a historical *occurrence*."[57] The resurrection is not ancillary to the personal identity enacted by Jesus prior to the crucifixion, but a real continuation of that life, and particularly of the decisions that led him to his powerlessness in passionate obedience to God. It is not "in the account of his person and teaching in his earlier ministry," but "directly in the passion-resurrection narrative" that his personal identity is revealed.[58] In the resurrection, Frei maintains, Jesus is most fully himself. Indeed, Jesus' identity, as manifested in this act of God, is "unsubstitutable" and "unique."[59]

The claim that Jesus is most himself in the resurrection sounds odd to modern ears. Perhaps this is because the wedge placed matter-of-factly between the Jesus of history and the Christ of faith in so much of post-Enlightenment exegesis even finds its way into expectations about how the scriptural narrative should be read. But if the reader respects scripture's own presentation of what Frei calls the "storied Jesus," realistically depicted in the Gospels from beginning to end, then the particularity of Jesus as a person, his very identity, extends from his early life to his resurrection and culminates, as does the story, in his passion and resurrection. Only in the terms set by the scriptural narrative's saving plot can the believer rightly appreciate both the particularity of the person Jesus Christ and the strength of his presence to and throughout history as the risen Lord. For he is, Frei affirms, "the one individual so completely himself that his inalienable identity not only points us to his own inescapable presence, but also is the focus toward which all of us orient our own identity— each one in his own person and place."[60]

Enacting the Story

This view of the particularity of Jesus manifested in biblical narrative has important implications for an understanding of Christian discipleship, as Stanley Hauerwas has suggested in many of his writings. The realistic pattern of scripture, he argues, is not just an accidental feature of the biblical text but "the narrative structure of Christian convictions for the life of the church."[61] That narrative structure becomes concrete not only in the shared profession of the church's faith but also in the ethical values believers affirm, the actions they undertake, and the character they build in conformity with the distinctiveness of the Christian story. For Hauerwas, the scriptural narrative does not offer one story among others, nor do the ethics of its lived story serve to justify the ethics of liberal society at large, or any other social organization for that matter. Rather, the church as an ethical community stands as an alternative to, and finally Hauerwas would say a judgment upon, other communities and the moral expectations they have of their members. The life of Christian discipleship involves the narrative-specific practice of "witnessing to the kind of social life possible for those that have been formed by the story of Christ."[62]

The particularity of Jesus is utterly central to the social ethic Hauerwas believes the church not merely to possess but actually to be. "Jesus," he claims, "is the story that forms the church."[63] The practice of that astounding claim entails nothing less than making Jesus' story one's own. Like Frei, whose intention-action analysis seeks to highlight the mutuality of Jesus' inner life and enacted ministry, Hauerwas insists that interpretation faithful to the Gospels' narrative framework is obliged to regard Jesus' person and work as inseparable.[64] The practice of Jesus' story in Christian discipleship cannot perfectly embody the unity of person and work that Jesus is. Being a disciple of Jesus cannot mean becoming Jesus. Such identification would annul both the particularity of Jesus, the source of his authority, and the status of discipleship, for which that authority remains normative. Yet the unity of Jesus' unsubstitutable person and work appears at least subordinately in the believer's formation of Christian character by the practiced enactment of the kingdom of God. One becomes a disciple by accepting Jesus' own narrative, a narrative of commitment to God's kingdom, as a pattern for one's own. And one grows in discipleship through the virtuous skill of making the innumerable stories of the world conform to the story of Jesus.[65]

Hauerwas's efforts to develop an ethics of the "storied Jesus" highlight themes that Frei did not make prominent in *The Identity of Jesus Christ* but of which he was by no means unaware. In fact, Frei brings his book to a close by reflecting on the life of the church and the meaning of Christian practice.

More than simply a witness to the presence of Christ in history, Frei claims, the church is itself "the public and communal form the indirect presence of Christ now takes, in contrast to his direct presence in his earthly days." As triumphalistically as such an ecclesiology might be understood, Frei offers this description only as an expression of Christian hope and as a modest reminder of the responsibilities of faithful discipleship. Like the risen Christ present in its midst, the church manifests its identity by acting upon its intentions. But the church does so, Frei insists, as a "follower," unable in its limitations, failures, and sinfulness to be "a complete reiteration of its Lord." As a "collective disciple," the church is called to narrate history not by eschatological specu- lation or prophecy but by word and deed, by the practice of the life of the savior.[66] Ever a theologian of grace, Frei presupposes that the practice of Christian discipleship is guided by the same divine providence portrayed in scriptural narration. Discipleship is finally the work of God. Yet, he concludes, "the name and identity of Jesus Christ, set forth in the narrative of the New Testament, call upon the believer for nothing less than this dis- cipleship."[67]

The Logical Integrity of Theology

In many respects, the various examples presented here as illus- trations of a nonfoundational approach to theology might seem too diverse to be ranked under a single rubric, no matter how general. This diversity is made even more complex because some of these illustrations offer their views by appealing explicitly to nonfoundational philosophy, while for others such appeal is only implicit and, for Barth at least, there seems to be no such appeal at all. Barth's undeniable influence on the development of non- foundational theology alone justifies his treatment here. But I would also argue that appeal to the views of nonfoundational philosophers is not necessary for the identification of a particular theologian's work as nonfoundational. What is necessary is that theological interpretation assess the nature, possibilities, and lim- itations of human knowledge in a manner consonant with the important critique of epistemology offered by thinkers like Witt- genstein, Quine, Rorty, and Davidson.

There are a number of ways in which this consonance can appear theologically. Like the philosophical criticism of the pre- tensions of modern epistemology, nonfoundational theologies reproach the way typically modern theologies privilege human subjectivity, as though some dimension of experiential immediacy offers an authoritative first principle or ground from which theological interpretation can reliably and justifiably proceed. Commitment to this extraordinarily dubious assumption has become so widespread in post-Enlightenment theology that, in the opinion of critics like Barth, Lindbeck, Thiemann, and Tanner, "modern" as it modifies "theology" is as much a negative value judgment as it is the delineation of a historical period. For them, modernity spans a time in which theological coherence, integrity, and intelligibility have been denied in the name of theology. In their works nonfoundational criticism serves, as it did for the philosophers, as a diagnostic aid for determining the symptoms of Cartesianism that by its prevalence has come to be regarded as the healthy norm rather than the epistemic malady it really is.

Like philosophers who understand knowledge as an intricate web of justifying explanations whose meaningfulness is relational, nonfoundational theologians understand the intelligibility of their claims to be rooted in the context of ecclesial belief, worship, and practice. In this holistic approach to theological knowledge, the apologetical enterprise of translation is suspect. Apologetics proceeds from the spurious assumption that the theoretical categories for translation elude the contexts between which they mediate, as though hypostatized conditions of certainty transcend the regional, lived settings in which knowledge actually flourishes. But even more basically, theologians like Lindbeck and Thiemann judge foundational theologies to err in their apparent assumption that the belief, worship, and practice of Christian tradition are insufficient to justify its theological claims. In the end, mediating theologians seem to be embarrassed by the contextuality of Christian belief and in their discomfort stand ready, as Frei points out, to forsake the self-referential character of its interpretation, as though Christian belief needed to refer to something other than itself in order to assure the possibility of its meaningfulness.

Like philosophers who judge the integrity of their own discipline to be vitiated by misconceptions about the workings of reason and the canons of logic, nonfoundational theologians excoriate understandings of their discipline that fail to respect the

logical integrity of theology. Foundationalists, they charge, suc-
cumb to the Cartesian anxiety by seeking closure to the task of
justifying theological claims. As different as the strategies to effect
this closure may be—from the appeal to immediate experience,
to reliance upon a putatively universal theory, to foundational
expectations of traditional syllogistic reasoning—all assume that
theology's logical integrity requires some determinate ground to
justify the extended complex of inferences that make a theological
argument, and that without such a grounding a theological argument will lose its coherence, cogency, and even rationality. For
nonfoundational theologians, these assumptions are foreign to
the ecclesial context in which the presuppositions, inferences,
and explanations of theological knowledge are shaped and within
which their validity is judged. Moreover, the logical indefensibility
of foundationalist assumptions outside the context of ecclesial
reasoning defeats the very purposes for which these assumptions
are used by mediating theologians. As William Placher has ob-
served, "If theologians try to defend their claims by starting with
basic, foundational truths that any rational person would have to
believe or observations independent of theory and assumption,
they are trying to do something that our best philosophers tell
us is impossible—not merely for religious beliefs but for any
beliefs whatever."[68]

Even though nonfoundational criticism in all its variety does
not propose any one alternative to traditional epistemology, metaphysics, and logic, it does offer some caveats about what knowledge and understanding are *not*. From a nonfoundational perspective, knowledge and understanding do not rest on principles
immediately experienced or certainly demonstrated, nor do they
appear as universal truths that lend themselves to regional translation. Knowledge and understanding are not independent of
context and its tightly woven fabric of epistemic, cultural, and
lived particularities, nor are the workings of reason that shape
knowledge and understanding context-free. Knowledge and understanding are not fixed points at the beginning or end of inferential justification, nor are they claims whose inferential pro-
liferation can be halted by their conspicuous truth. Applying these
creative denials to theology's pursuit of knowledge and understanding yields interesting and, to be sure, relative criteria for
the logical integrity of its undertaking.

Rather than expecting theological reasoning to offer reflection on faith based on a context other than its own or on a transcendental truth free of any context, a nonfoundational approach to theology would recognize the disciplinary commitments of reason. Disciplines, after all, are contextually bound, as well as contexts in their own right. They are products of particular times and places, as the conduct of their practitioners throughout their respective histories clearly demonstrates. More importantly, as contexts themselves disciplines have expectations for the workings of reasoning that reflect their own assumptions, concerns, purposes, and values. Nonfoundational criticism may have originated in the discipline of philosophy, but its epistemic analysis has implications for all disciplines, including theology. Theological reasoning is not a regional application of a universal operation of consciousness, self-identical in all human beings. Like all actual modes of reflection, theological reasoning is one of many particular operations from which the lifeless abstraction of reasoning itself might be, but is better not, culled. And like all actual modes of reflection, theological reasoning is woven into a context, in its case an ecclesial framework of scripture, belief, practice, and even interpretation by which it is informed and which it in turn forms.

As Charles Wood has noted, "the conditions of Christian understanding" suggest "that 'understanding' is less aptly characterized as *phenomenon* than as *ability*—to the extent that any general characterization of it may succeed."[69] By this distinction, Wood intends to press home the point that Christian understanding, or any act of understanding for that matter, is not primarily a subjective event but a functional set of practices cultivated in determinate circumstances. Theological reasoning is a specific example of that ability. For its practice to be meaningful or illuminating or edifying it must at least begin its interpretation by faithfulness to the contextuality of the faith lived by the church. In this chapter we have seen the contextuality of theological reasoning portrayed in several ways, from Frei's attention to the Bible's realistic narrative, to Lindbeck's understanding of the doctrinally regulated tradition, to Thiemann's highlighting of the promissory cast of scriptural language. Finally, though, these are but nuanced depictions of the priority, and hence authority, of the Christian message of graceful salvation for the practice of theological reasoning. For nonfoundationalists, theological reasoning that shirks its responsibilities to this centuries-old context of meaning or that ignores its inseparability from this context simply does not recognize its priorities.

In some quarters this conception of interpretive ability might seem parochial. Yet nonfoundational theologians do not argue that theology's interpretive directions need be limited to the ecclesial setting from which they issue. Nonfoundational interpretation can assess cultural life and political issues. It can address the enduring human problems of racism, injustice, and poverty. It can shed light on the most recent advances in medical technology or on our knowledge of the evolution of the cosmos. Nonfoundational interpretation can, in short, examine any of the themes or topics that have been considered the property of foundational theologies in the modern period.

Nonfoundational interpretation, however, insists on the logical integrity of theology, which it understands as faithfulness to its central beliefs in the very process of its inferential reasoning. Inferential reasoning, in other words, must always *defer* in the movement of its logic to Christian claims about God, Christ, and salvation if it is to be truly theological. Theological inference may engage in this logical deference by insisting with Frei on the priority of Jesus' identity to his presence, or by standing ready with Tanner to counter the prevalence of foundational reasoning in modern theology, or with Lindbeck by abiding by the intratextuality of Christian interpretation. Whatever interpretive heuristic a theology invokes is appropriate to the degree that it assures the coherence of its reasoning from inference to inference. Only through such coherence, nonfoundationalists assert, can theology be authentically credible and truly cogent. And only through the contextuality of its own disciplinary reasoning can theology assure its own logical integrity.

3

Nonfoundational Theology in Critical Perspective

We may be inclined to think of Christian theology as though it were a singular something, a discipline uniform in method or interpretive style and devoted to acknowledged canons for its proper conduct. What we call Christian theology is actually the history of many interpretive approaches seeking the intelligibility of a religious tradition that is itself denominationally, culturally, and, of course, personally diverse. Nonfoundational theology has appeared recently in this pluralistic history. Its own modernity, however, is a source of ambivalence within its interpretive project—an issue to be confronted rather than simply a marker in the temporal scheme of things. From one point of view, nonfoundational theology looks like a recent contribution to the tradition's interpretive pluralism, but from another it is a response to, and a negative judgment upon, recent theological pluralism. From one point of view, nonfoundational theology seems committed to the insights of the latest developments in philosophy, but from another it offers an approach to theological interpretation that is utterly traditional and in some respects even premodern in its sensibilities. From one point of view, nonfoundational theology seems dissatisfied with the character of modern or post-Enlightenment theology, but from another it is undeniably modern in its interpretive presuppositions. While some might regard these juxtapositions as inconsistencies, I think it would be fairer to view them as manifestations of a complex, paradoxical character, and one that promises to influence modern theology for many years to come.

There is a tendency on the part of nonfoundational theologians to represent modern theology pejoratively, as a counterpoint to their own commendations for right interpretation. Were we to understand modern theology, though, not merely as foundational apologetics but in terms of its practitioners' commitment to a broad set of disciplinary assumptions, nonfoundational theology would certainly be counted as a type of modern theology. Modern theology affirms the legitimacy of historical-critical interpretations of scripture and tradition and eagerly parts company with fundamentalistic naiveté. Modern theology wrestles in some way with the Enlightenment's challenge to traditional authority and the anthropological orientation of its claims for truth. And modern theology affirms the historicity of its truth-claims, expressed in the idea of the development of doctrine and the theologian's creative role in fostering that development by the exercise of insight and imagination. While nonfoundational theology fits the profile of theology's modern assumptions, it remains uncomfortable with how those assumptions have been and continue to be enacted in the post-Enlightenment period. This discomfort, however, is the unease of disappointment, and not despair or rejection. If the character of nonfoundational theology can be described as paradoxical, then both its grave misgivings about modern interpretive practice and its hope that the same practice can be properly reformed pose the dilemma of its hermeneutical identity.[1]

In this last chapter we will continue to explore nonfoundational theology's program for interpretive reform by examining more closely a number of themes suggested by our discussion thus far. Since our space is limited, our analysis cannot be exhaustive. Our treatment of nonfoundationalism in the following pages will be more critical than descriptive in its perspective. We will consider in turn the metaphorical character of nonfoundational discourse, the nature of theological reasoning, the problem of exclusivity for a nonfoundational theology, and finally the promise of the nonfoundational approach for theological interpretation.

Contextual Consistency and the
Metaphor of "Foundations"

One of the issues that always seems to be raised in a consideration of nonfoundationalism, whether as philosophical criticism or as theological interpretation, is the nature of the "foundations" that foundationalism affirms and nonfoundationalism denies. For some, there remains something startling and even disconcerting about the idea that epistemic claims do not possess foundations. At a certain level that position evokes the expectation of a skepticism so radical that it cannot escape the pitfalls of nihilism and moral indifference. None of the nonfoundational philosophers we have considered, however, argues to these conclusions. Indeed, philosophers like Willard Quine, Wilfrid Sellars, and Richard Rorty are preoccupied with the nature of epistemic claims and not with their possibility, which in typically pragmatic fashion they seem to take for granted. Nevertheless, critics of nonfoundationalism often fear that nihilism is the necessary consequence of epistemic relativism and so seize every opportunity to argue that such relativism is logically self-defeating. Nonfoundationalists, the criticism goes, may condemn a particular notion of foundations for knowledge, but the commitment to meaning or action requires some foundational presupposition, however it be understood. While nonfoundationalists dismiss this judgment as an expression of what Richard Bernstein calls "Cartesian anxiety," there is something telling in the criticism that can be helpful in understanding the notion of foundations. That telling point does not diminish the cogency of the nonfoundational position. It does, though, call attention to the faithfulness of even the rhetoric of nonfoundationalism to the contextuality of knowledge for which it argues.

The Trope of "Foundations"

Foundationalists might argue that nonfoundationalists cannot avoid appeal to some authoritative givenness that functions as an epistemic assumption in their understanding of justifying belief. Quine, for example, may decry foundational expectations of theorizing. But his holistic understanding of knowledge reflects his own behavioristic assumptions about the workings of human experience. Rorty may reject the Western tradition's common assumption that immediately caused acts of knowing ground knowledge in general. But he accepts that tradition's ancient, and largely Platonic, assumption that authentic knowing is reached through critical dialogue. Michael Williams may chide foundationalists for their groundless concern about an infinite justificatory regress. But his argument against the significance of the regress cannot transcend Western logic's most basic premise about the linear character of reasoning. Nevertheless, as much as critics of nonfoundationalism assert that such assumptions evince the inescapability of foundationalism, their criticism finally misses the mark. Nonfoundationalists, after all, do not claim that explanations should or can transcend assumptions, but only that no privileged assumption possesses the ability to ground the edifice of knowledge. Nor, they argue, is such a privileged assumption needed for knowledge to be meaningful. Nonfoundationalists would readily admit that knowledge appeals to a host of background beliefs—assumptions, we might say—that provide a context for explanation. That context, however, is indeterminate, and ever resistant to the closure that the foundationalist seeks. The foundationalist who delights in the nonfoundationalist's inconsistency by finding "foundations" in the assumptions that permeate the network of belief misunderstands how the conception of foundations functions in nonfoundational criticism. This misunderstanding, however, does illuminate a rhetorical dimension of the nonfoundational argument easily missed in the rigor (and the jargon!) of sophisticated philosophical analysis.

Nonfoundational philosophers use the term *foundations* as a metaphor to depict epistemic presuppositions imbued with far more authority than can be warranted by the evidence of experience, the exercise of reasoning, or the consistent application of the rules of traditional logic. "Foundations" for knowledge can be described as universal and so undebatable principles of argumentation, or as a justifying belief itself not in need of justification, or as an immediately available, universal, and noninferential mode of knowing to which other claims must appeal for their validity. However differently foundations be portrayed, their defenders all err in a similar way by according extraordinary privilege to what is no more than an assumption about how beliefs are justified. Nonfoundationalists tend, then, to use the metaphor of foundations to describe a particular conception of authoritative givenness—one that wrongly presumes that the process of justifying belief can reach logical closure in a universally available truth, and that this logical closure is necessary for the truth of the body of knowledge it supports. Arguing as the foundationalist does—that the inescapability of assumptions in the course of philosophical explanation demonstrates the inconsistency of the nonfoundational position—fails to appreciate the metaphorical character of foundations in nonfoundational discourse. At the same time, this misguided argument highlights the degree to which "foundations" is indeed a trope that is meaningful when used in certain ways and meaningless when used in others. The metaphorical character of this epistemic rhetoric can be illustrated by exploring the distinction some philosophers make between "strong" and "weak" forms of foundationalism.

The criticism of foundationalism has been so compelling that a consensus has emerged among philosophers regarding the inability of reasoning to demonstrate foundations for knowledge by the epistemological strategies of rationalism or empiricism. The prospect of an infinite regress in the justification of belief, however, has led some philosophers to seek a middle ground between the cogency of the nonfoundational position and the felt need to maintain at least the *possibility* of some notion of foundationalism. William Alston, for example, has distinguished between what he calls "iterative" and "simple" foundationalism. Alston is quite willing to concede that an iterative foundation for knowledge, one self-certain or demonstrable, is beyond the power of reasoning. But, he insists, there must be a "*stock* of directly justified beliefs" constituting a foundation for the network of beliefs if acts of knowing are to possess any integrity.[2] One cannot construct knowledge logically on the basis of such directly justified beliefs. But at least postulating their existence accounts for the warrants we ascribe to some beliefs and not to others, and explains the credibility of any justified belief. For Alston, simple or "weak" foundations may be incapable of demonstration, but their existence, if only as hypothetical postulates, cannot be disproved.[3] The advantage of simple foundationalism is that it offers the best of both philosophical stances: "one can stop the regress of justification" by maintaining the possibility of a stock of immediately justified beliefs, and do so "without falling into [the] dogmatism" of strong or iterative foundationalism.[4]

One finds Alston's general distinction made in a number of ways in the literature of the foundations debate. Whether one speaks of minimal and maximal,[5] or formal and substantive,[6] or soft and hard[7] forms of foundationalism, the purpose of the distinction is the same. Those who would defend a weak (simple, minimal, formal, soft) foundationalism would acknowledge the cogency of the arguments against a strong (iterative, maximal, substantive, hard) foundationalism, but would be unwilling to sacrifice the metaphor of foundations completely. Alston, we noted, applies the metaphor of foundations to the stock of beliefs that are basic to our warranted judgments. But aside from Alston's unprovable assertion that they *can* be directly justified, this fund of beliefs is really no different from the background beliefs that his critics would regard as the foundationless context for any act of knowing. Whereas philosophers like Alston would distribute foundational authority amid the network of belief in immediately justified (albeit hypothetical) postulates, philosophers like Quine and Davidson would relinquish foundations altogether and rest content with the sheer contextuality of the same network. Both parties would acknowledge the workings of assumptions in the network of belief. Weak foundationalists, however, would preserve the metaphor of foundations to name the authority of supposedly privileged assumptions that they consider, at least in theory, to be epistemically important. For nonfoundationalists, on the contrary, a foundation by any name would be as illusory. Either weak foundationalism is a guise for the strong variety that all parties agree is logically untenable, or it is so weak that it is no foundation at all and really just the indeterminate stock of contextual beliefs accompanying any particular belief.[8] Simply put, the metaphor can flourish in distinctions or be lost in negation depending on the philosophical commitments of its user.

The Trope of "Nonfoundational"

Whatever residues of dogmatism appear in the views of the weak foundationalist, he or she, by virtue of rather desperate logical contortions and forced distinctions, is perhaps better aware than anyone of the rhetorical dimension of the foundations debate. Ironically, it is the nonfoundationalist who might be a bit uneasy about the claim that "foundations" functions as a metaphor in nonfoundational discourse. If "foundations" is a metaphor, then so too is the absence of foundations for which nonfoundational criticism argues. To the degree that the nonfoundationalist regards his or her position as a description of the workings of knowledge, the prospect of regarding both "foundations" and the "absence of foundations" as metaphors might seem to compromise the very integrity of his or her explanation or perhaps to justify the foundationalist's charge of epistemic nihilism. Indeed, the nonfoundationalist's uneasiness in the face of the metaphorical character of his or her own discourse might be a manifestation of the same Cartesian anxiety that plagues the foundationalist's efforts to justify belief. Metaphors, by their very nature, instantiate language's relativity. As consistent as the nonfoundational argument may be against the logical viability of foundations for knowledge, there remains a temptation in nonfoundational discourse to regard the counter-metaphor of "foundationlessness" as oddly impervious to the very relativity it expresses and so as no metaphor at all. But what could foundationlessness possibly be were it not a metaphor, an image tied in its use to another image (in this case, most strikingly, its opposite) and deriving its meaning, as Davidson would say, from nothing but that use?[9]

The point of this rhetorical question is that nonfoundational discourse is itself an expression of the utter contextuality of knowledge for which it argues, and that its use of metaphors to describe epistemological problems and their solutions is a matter of pragmatic choice within, and expressive of, that same contextuality. Used in philosophical discourse to name and to unname epistemic claims, the metaphor of "foundationlessness" has the capacity to present the relativity of epistemic structures in a way that rivals the best of detailed arguments. Its use, however, is neither generic nor neutral nor expressive of metaphysical essences or vacuums, but rather a particular claim about the inadequacy of a particular claim. As accustomed as one might be to the use of metaphor in poetry, literature, and common parlance, its use in philosophy, as Rorty's work has demonstrated, often remains unexamined, a dimension of philosophical argument that passes unappreciated. The same, I would suggest, is true of the use of metaphor in theology.

Posing the Issues Theologically

Like their philosophical counterparts, nonfoundational theologians use the metaphors of "foundations" and "foundationlessness" in particular ways, and these specific uses reflect value judgments about what is deemed theologically problematic and theologically appropriate. The nonfoundational theologians examined in chapter 2 use the metaphor of foundations to name an extrabiblical theory or a supposedly universal human experience that such a theory purports to represent. For nonfoundationalists, the theological appeal to extrabiblical theory wrongly accepts the Enlightenment and post-Enlightenment assumption that the biblical text possesses at most a meaning that lies beyond the scope of its own narrative content, as though the categories of the scriptural narrative stand in need of theoretical translation for their meaningfulness to crystalize. The Christian faith, they insist, possesses its own contextuality (in Quine's terms, a set of background beliefs) in its scriptural writings, doctrines, liturgical practices, community life, and committed behavior. Theological reflection must find its meaning, determine its aims, and conduct its analysis within this context if it is to be faithful to its task. The apologetical enterprise encourages theology to set its purposes as though Christian faith were not shaped, preached, and enacted within such a context or as though its own context begged for a superior intelligibility in another.

The foundations, then, that nonfoundational theologians regard as problematic are, most generally expressed, contexts of meaning other than Christian belief and practice accorded interpretive primacy over the Christian context of meaning. Or, to express the same idea from the perspective of foundationalist aspirations, the foundations that nonfoundational theologians judge to be problematic are views, principles, or theories regarded as context-free and so universally meaningful beyond any regional context of meaning, Christianity's included. Defining the theological use of the metaphor of foundations thus, as any universal theory put to the service of apologetics, brings into relief how nonfoundational theologians choose *not* to use the metaphor. Better put, the closer definition of the metaphor highlights the way nonfoundational theologians choose to apply the metaphors of "nonfoundation" or "foundationlessness." *Foundationlessness* in the work of theologians like George Lindbeck, Ronald Thiemann, and Stanley Hauerwas refers to Christian faith as it has been normatively expressed, practiced, and experienced through the ages. While the normatively Christian can be encountered in the devotion, words, or actions of believers, it is most surely met in the scriptural writings that Christian tradition has affirmed as God's revelation, and in the doctrinal statements that provide guidelines for the right reading and living of scripture. *Foundationlessness*, then, names the web of practiced Christian belief faithful to the norms shaped by its ecclesial life. Or, negatively expressed, it names Christian belief defined not by some other meaningful particularity, but by its own.

This attention to nonfoundational metaphors makes us more keenly aware of their limitations. The nonfoundational philosophers we have examined, for instance, hardly would accept the theological conception of "foundationlessness" delineated in the work of Lindbeck and Thiemann. For the philosophers, any appeal to the revelational authority of a religious tradition would constitute a foundationalism that warranted reasoning could not abide. From Paul's claim that the preaching of Christ crucified is foolishness to the Greeks (1 Cor. 1:23) to contemporary theological defenses against the attacks of philosophers of religion, Christians have conceded in so many words that faith in God's revelation cannot be justified reasonably beyond the circle of faith. Nonfoundational philosophers would call such a claim an immediately justified belief. In fact, philosophers like Quine, Sellars, and Rorty limit their criticism of foundationalism to its various empiricist and rationalist varieties. Their unwillingness to raise their critical voices against theological claims, however, cannot be attributed to their high regard for the foundationlessness of Christian contextuality but to their judgment that the authoritative claims of faith are examples of a foundationalism too obvious to refute.

I make this point not to suggest that nonfoundational theology is a contradiction in terms but to stress just how contextually bound is any perspective on nonfoundational meaning and the foundationalism against which it defines itself. A nonfoundational argument developed in the interests of either philosophy or theology can be faithful both to those interests and to the groundlessness of knowledge only if it presents its case particularly, with respect to the background beliefs that it claims as its own. Even the key metaphors invoked in a nonfoundational argument fall within the scope of its background beliefs. The metaphors of foundation and foundationlessness specify neither a context-free error nor a context-free epistemic norm respectively. Their meaning is a function of their use, a use made in a certain setting on behalf of certain values. In other words, the limitations of the metaphors invoked in a nonfoundational argument are not expressions of their weakness but of the legitimate contextual consistency for which nonfoundationalists argue, whether they be philosophers or theologians. Nonfoundational theologians learn much from philosophers like Quine, Rorty, and Davidson about the nature of reasoning, the vain attractions of universal theories, and the contextuality of knowledge. But were the theologians simply to accept the arguments of the philosophers in the philosophers' own terms, they would negate both their own background beliefs and the particularity that nonfoundational argumentation expects.

That theologians would adapt a philosophical position to express their own concerns is hardly surprising and, as we have seen, a strategy as old as Christian theological reflection itself. Nonfoundational philosophy's own expectation of contextual consistency encourages this theological procedure, even if the nonfoundational philosophers are indifferent to the discipline of theology and the value of its knowledge. The same contextuality of Christian belief that warrants this strategy of adaptation, however, also has implications for how nonfoundational theologians are obliged to make their arguments.

Confessional Styles of Criticism

Thus far in our discussion the context from which nonfoundational theologians argue has been described as Christian and identified with that religious tradition's scriptures, doctrines, practices, and beliefs. Nonfoundational theologians can, and often do, seek the understanding of faith at this most generic level of the Christian as such. But Christianity is characterized by a rich diversity of confessions, each marked by its particular way of reading scripture, doctrinal commitments, view of ecclesial authority, and prescriptions for Christian living. As much as Christians speak of the Christian as such, their discourse eventually is shaped by the background beliefs that define the confession in which they stand. The discourse of Christian theologians is no different, a point the nonfoundational theologian should be especially disposed to appreciate. If nonfoundational theology is to be consistent in its claims for the contextuality of knowledge, then its disciplinary reception of the insights of the philosophers must be completed by a confessional reception keenly aware of how thick the web of Christian particularity may actually be, and so of how nuanced the use of the metaphors of "foundations" and "foundationlessness" might need to be if their meaningfulness is to reflect the background beliefs of the confession they describe.

Theologians who have heralded the value of a nonfoundational approach to theology—Frei, Lindbeck, Thiemann, and Tanner, among others—have largely developed their arguments from the perspective of Protestant confessions. Their insistence on the priority of the scriptural narrative, their antipathy to speculation as an aid to theological reasoning, and their commitment to a descriptive or, broadly speaking, exegetical approach to theological interpretation bespeak the extent to which the confessional sensibilities of classical Protestantism shape the conception of foundationlessness they consider to be normative. Moreover, the conception of foundations that these theologians find problematic is defined in opposition to these background beliefs and so is characterized, albeit negatively, by the same confessional sensibilities that mold their understanding of theological norms. At the level of the most generally Christian, and so irrespective of confessional commitment, one might say that the foundations that the theologians examined in the previous chapter judge to be spurious is any accordance of priority to the human over the divine. But the particular ways in which this illegitimate prioritizing is conceived—as the privileging of experience over the

Word, the speculation involved in the apologetical enterprise, and (we might even say) as a conception of theologizing in which human "works" vainly aspire to a *theologia gloriae*—all evince a contextuality configured by the doctrines of classical Protestantism.

I would not judge the Protestant contextuality of nonfoundational theologians like Frei, Lindbeck, Thiemann, and Tanner to be a weakness. Indeed, the previous paragraphs have delineated an argument for contextual consistency in nonfoundational interpretation that appreciates just how finely the web of foundationless belief is woven in confessional, as well as in disciplinary, strands. The consistency between their insightful criticism of foundationalist pretensions and the particularity of their confessional beliefs is one of the many strengths of the Protestant nonfoundationalists. But because these theologians tend not to explicate their confessional commitments directly as they criticize modern apologetics, they open themselves to a reading in which the metaphors of "foundations" and "foundationlessness" are regarded as universally Christian judgments naming the theologically false and the theologically true, without regard for the confessional contexts in which these judgments are inevitably made. To the degree that Protestant theologians sharing both similar confessional commitments and similar views about the problematic nature of modern theology have been the most influential advocates of nonfoundational theological interpretation, this reading is all the easier to advance.

If nonfoundational interpretation is truly to receive the theological appreciation it deserves, then its mandate for contextual consistency must be heeded in the most nuanced ways possible. Nonfoundational criticism put to the service of theology encourages reflection on the faith keenly aware of faith's particularity. Nonfoundational criticism remains on guard against reasoning's proclivity to ignore the contextuality of its own background beliefs and the role played by those beliefs in shaping the workings of reasoning itself. And nonfoundational criticism identifies justifications of belief that claim authority they could never possess, and by exposing the groundlessness of purportedly epistemic foundations enacts its commitment to the wider circle of mutually defined assumptions, beliefs, and practices that it holds as its own. The theological practitioner of such criticism, however, must not lose sight of the fact that the Christian context nonfoundationally identified and protected from the encroachments of false principles is remarkably differentiated. While there are background beliefs that all Christian confessions share (like the doctrine of creation, the doctrine of the divinity and humanity of Jesus, and the doctrine of the saving power of Christ's resurrection), their confessional relations to other more particular Christian beliefs (like the irresistibility of divine grace, papal infallibility, and the unacceptability of the *filioque*) subtly, and at times even dramatically, contextualize even their most apparently general claims.

The contextual consistency to which nonfoundational criticism is committed requires that theological versions of that criticism respect the nuanced particularities of the Christian tradition expressed in its various confessional claims. This diversity calls for a more differentiated use of nonfoundational metaphors than invoked in the work of the theologians we have examined. As we have seen, the theologians considered in the previous chapter largely use the metaphor of foundations to characterize modern apologetical theories because they judge the values of those theories to be antithetical to the background beliefs of classical Protestantism. A Roman Catholic understanding of foundations conceived in light of the teachings of the Second Vatican Council, however, might not find modern apologetics to be nearly as problematic within its own context as an exclusively institutional view of church and ecclesial authority, or its tendency to neglect the centrality of scripture to the life of the church, or its older method of Denzinger theology in which reason ahistorically and uncritically justifies magisterial teachings. A Protestant conception of foundationlessness would certainly affirm the value of scriptural narrative as practiced in the communal life of Christian discipleship. A Roman Catholic use of the same metaphor would define the contextuality of belief by reference to a wider narrative encompassing both scripture and a normative tradition that classical Protestantism would be unwilling to recognize as authoritative.

Those uncomfortable with nonfoundational theologies might view these rhetorical particularities as expressions of confessional exclusivisms too parochial to be of theological value. That discomfort, however, probably stems from the expectation that theology's first responsibility is to justify its claims to the culture at large. Nonfoundational theologians count apologetics as a theological responsibility. It is not, however, one that has priority. From a nonfoundational perspective, the first responsibility of theology is to its own identity, which has shown signs of continual erosion in the modern age. The metaphorical nuances between which one can and should distinguish in the rhetoric of nonfoundational theologies are expressions of the priority that Christian confessions need to accord to their own background beliefs if their arguments are to be both contextually consistent and, in particular circumstances, apologetically cogent.

Reasoning and Christian Identity

Nonfoundational criticism possesses interesting implications for virtually all of the *loci* or areas that theology might address. We have already considered several of these. The authority of scripture and tradition, sin and grace, ecclesiology, christology, and the Christian life are some of the topics addressed from a nonfoundational perspective by the theologians we have examined. An issue attending these topics but not treated explicitly thus far is the nature of the theological reasoning that reflects on faith, offers explanations of Christian meaning, and criticizes foundational claims in the network of belief. If the claims that Christian confessions regard as authoritative are as contextually particular as the nonfoundational perspective suggests, then could the reasoning that investigates these claims stand apart from that context, as though its own powers were uninfluenced by the background beliefs it examines? At first, the consequences of giving anything but an affirmative answer to this question seem startling. One expects reasoning to be neutral and able to conduct its analysis apart from any context. Its power to discriminate judiciously, one would think, would be impaired or even vitiated by the contextualization of its activity. Nonfoundational criticism may offer valuable insights into the contextuality of knowledge. But if that contextuality extends to the activity of reasoning itself, how would the powers of reflection, analysis, construction, and criticism be able to offer more than a circular reiteration of reasoning's background beliefs?

It is important to address the concerns raised in these questions, if only to point out the foundationalist expectations of reasoning they express. A nonfoundational approach to logical analysis certainly would not advocate circular reasoning. Nor would it advocate conducting its affairs indiscriminately, by its own self-understanding unable to adjudicate between its claims and others. The apprehension that these most basic flaws of inquiry would be the inescapable consequences of a contextual understanding of reasoning reflects the Cartesian assumptions of the interrogator much more than it fathoms any inherent deficiencies in the nonfoundational view. To the degree that reasoning is always the reasoning of this person or that, with these beliefs or those, in this culture or that, in this time or another, it remains very much an activity tied to particular systems of meaning, both informed by the claims it values and functionally committed to those claims in its own workings. Cartesianism in its many forms has encouraged moderns to conceive of reasonable inquiry as a disinterested activity, impervious to influence from any quarter and committed only to founded conclusions that show themselves to be justified in the course of a completely value-free investigation. This conceptualization admirably promulgates the virtues of open-mindedness, judiciousness, and the free pursuit of truth expected in all rational investigation. Its supposition, however, that these virtues are exclusively compatible with a context-free, universal reasoning is an unjustified belief, a privileged claim that fails to recognize the value-laden activity that reasoning is.

Perhaps it is this modern notion of universal reasoning that discourages the understanding of reasoning as a practice located within specific contexts of meaning. Reasoning possesses a physiological aspect which, at least minimalistically, functions the same in all. Reasoning can be regulated in certain styles of logic or argumentation whose sense can be recognized by many cultures though they be the product of one. Reasoning, however, is a human activity. And even though the human may be conceptualized in the most universal terms possible, its meaningfulness is finally a function of its use, the sum of the practiced values that men and women make real in their individual and communal lives. Reasoning can only stand within that framework of beliefs and practices, for there is no extracontextual alternative. Within that framework its activity *is* a belief and a practice which, when self-aware and consistent, serves its commitment to its contextual values. This nonfoundational assessment of reasoning applies as much to its theological practice as it does to any other, a point argued cogently by Nicholas Wolterstorff in his book *Reason within the Bounds of Religion* (1976).

Foundationalism, Wolterstorff contends, has shown itself to be a deficient theory of theorizing. Its expectation that the truth of propositions finally be justified noninferentially and with certitude fails its own epistemic litmus test. Although claims for such certitude frequently have been made in the history of thought, the disagreements among the many claimants suggest that one person's certitude is another's doubt. A foundationalist theory of knowledge, Wolterstorff points out, also would require an unrealizable number of indubitable propositions to justify belief universally in the actual circumstances of life. Even the most simple statement of observation, however, would encounter enough discrepancies, quibbles, and qualifications among experiencers to preclude the possibility of such indubitable assent. If foundationalism is an inadequate theory of knowledge, then Christian reasoning, whether at work in daily life or in theological interpretation, must reject its approach to the justification of belief.

Like most nonfoundationalists, Wolterstorff readily concedes that there is a stock of beliefs without which theorizing of any sort would be impossible. These "data-background beliefs" are not foundations for knowledge. They present no evidence for their certainty, nor do they necessarily support other beliefs. Such nonfoundational assumptions may show themselves to be problematic and subject to criticism, revision, and even rejection on virtually any occasion. But on the occasion of "weighing . . . a given theory at a given time all such data-background theories are taken as unproblematic."[10] At such moments of judgment, data-background theories function as what Wolterstorff calls "control beliefs" or specific "beliefs as to what constitutes an acceptable *sort* of theory on the matter under consideration."[11] Control beliefs adjudicate between theories both positively and negatively.

On the one hand, they encourage the formation of theories consistent with one's beliefs; on the other, they reject theories that lack such consistency or that though consistent with those beliefs do not offer a satisfactory explanation of the data. In Wolterstorff's view, then, control beliefs neither lead to circular reasoning nor are determinative of the theories our knowledge comprises. They are open to modification throughout most of our experience, and even in the moment of adjudication theories must yield to the evidence they explain. Control beliefs offer a nonfoundational heuristic to guide inquiry and pose the actual framework within which inquiry proceeds.

Among the many beliefs that adjudicate theory, one would expect the religious beliefs of a person so committed to be especially important. Indeed, the "religious beliefs of the Christian scholar," Wolterstorff insists, "ought to function as *control* beliefs within his devising and weighing of theories."[12] Religious beliefs put to such practice would not have exclusive power to fix the standards of contextual consistency. Exclusivity of that sort would constitute the variety of foundationalism usually called fundamentalism. Rationalist or empiricist versions of foundationalism, however, would exclude religious beliefs from any controlling role in the assessment of theories, their very particularity failing to meet the foundationalist's universal criterion of justification. This exclusion would be both arbitrary and hypothetical—the former because there is no evidence for the validity or even possibility of a universal norm of justification, the latter because the foundationalist must simply ignore the actual ways the beliefs of religious people seek compatible theories. Christians would not be surprised by the claim that their commitment calls for enactment in every aspect of their lives if their faith is real. That exhortation is implicit in every scriptural passage, explicit in every credible sermon, and the voice of any conscience faithful to the gospel. Extending that claim to reasoning, even to the reasoning involved in theological interpretation, might seem parochial to foundationalist sensibilities. For Wolterstorff, though, religious reasoning is a meaningful practice among the many practices by which reasoning might be enacted, and one required by the content of Christian belief itself.

By emphasizing the contextuality of reasoning, Wolterstorff rejects the Enlightenment view that reason transcends contexts, hovering, as it were, above them and from some imagined neutral position evaluating their particular and so, from its own foundationalist perspective, prejudiced claims. If religious commitment is an important context for reasoning, then religious reasoning, from pious reflection to theological analysis, is a practice like reading the scriptures for spiritual edification, reception of the sacraments, or observance of holy days. Nonfoundationalists like Wolterstorff do not present their account of the nature of reasoning as a constructive revision of this activity, but as a description of how reasoning has always functioned. Were one to consider the history of theology in light of this claim, the results would be illuminating.

Much of Christian theology has invested the authority of its logical argumentation in foundationalist assumptions about the justification of belief. Theology was not alone in making this investment. To the degree that Western culture has shaped its understanding of justified belief along lines set by the classical philosophical tradition, its disciplinary approaches to knowledge, including the newest arrivals in the natural and social sciences, have largely embraced the foundationalist model. Theology, however, traditionally has defined its disciplinary priorities differently from the other sciences. By conceiving its enterprise as faith seeking understanding, theology marks its commitment to an authority that supersedes any foundation within the scope of reason or its attendant experiences. From the standpoint of philosophical reason, according such priority to faith may seem to be the most blatant example of foundationalism, since it claims privilege for a belief beyond reasonable analysis. But within theology's own context of meaning, faith seeking understanding well expresses the priority of contextual meaning expected by nonfoundational criticism of any exercise of reasoning. In Wolterstorff's terminology, this classical definition of theology insists that faith functions as a control belief in selecting configurations of understanding (theories, he would say) consistent with its values.

Wolterstorff's understanding of Christian reasoning coincides with the view of theological integrity suggested at the end of the previous chapter. A nonfoundational theology would practice inferential reasoning in a manner faithful to the central beliefs of the tradition, deferring at every step in its logical path to the authority of those beliefs and by such deference enacting their claims. This view of inference as deference may suggest a conceptualization of logical coherence too narrow to avoid the fideism of which nonfoundational theology is sometimes accused.[13] While fideism remains a pitfall for nonfoundational theology to avoid, its interpretive commitments by no means lead necessarily to this religious version of foundationalism against which its own critical tenets stand guard. Theological reasoning deferential to the contextuality of its belief can, and indeed must, argue beyond its meaningful framework if its arguments are to address the personal and public circumstances of those inside and outside the church. Theological reasoning must do justice to the plethora of evidence that arises in the course of our common history, shaped as it is by the words and deeds of individuals, groups, and nations. Loyalty, however, to Christian identity remains the first responsibility of theological interpretation and the reasoning by which it is accomplished.

Theological Particularity and the Problem of Exclusivity

However often theology has appealed to foundationalist theories in its analytical efforts to bring understanding to faith, its most typical disciplinary self-understanding has been compatible with the nonfoundational perspective. Theology, one might say, has been nonfoundational throughout its history, in its aim if not in its execution. Theologians, then, should be inclined toward the perspective of nonfoundational criticism as a way of understanding how reasoning in their discipline not only actually does but also should work. Nonfoundational theology has appeared as an explicit interpretive approach only in recent years. Relatively few theologians, however, have been willing to adopt its perspective. Chief among the reasons for this reluctance is the concern that a nonfoundational theology is too exclusive in its interpretive sensibilities, by its rejection of modern apologetics unable to offer judgments beyond its confessional scope. Our discussion of the workings of nonfoundational theological inference has shown this concern to be baseless. Arguing as nonfoundationalists do, that theological inference should defer in its logic to the meaningful context of Christian belief, does not entail the restriction of reasoning to that context. Reasoning's loyalty to its values does not entail a narrowness in its scope.

Room for Difference?

Even if this answer is convincing, the problem of exclusivity might seem to abide in the methodological commitments of nonfoundational theologians. The theologians we have examined all commend description as the appropriate procedure for their discipline and castigate theological speculation as an enterprise foundationalist in its inclinations. This uniformity in approach does much to confirm the fear that nonfoundational theologies are restrictive in practice, the particularity they urge limiting the range of approaches able to be methodologically faithful to Christian belief. Not surprisingly, descriptive forms of theology have been the first to carry the banner of nonfoundationalism into their discipline. The Protestant reformers made exegesis the model of theological interpretation, conceiving of the theologian's work as the faithful exposition of the plain sense of scripture. Their disdain for speculative approaches to theology expressed their judgment that a metaphysically inclined reasoning all too often substituted its own claims for those of divine revelation. These sensibilities conform well to the sort of criticism advanced by nonfoundationalism, and modern standard-bearers of those classical Protestant sensibilities have perceived its value for promulgating faithfulness to the Christian particularity they judge to be threatened in the modern age.

It would be important to consider whether speculative approaches to interpretation that take shape, for example, as existentialist, transcendental, and process theologies can be conducted in a nonfoundational manner. Applied philosophically, nonfoundational criticism finds reason's speculative forays to be beyond its real abilities and falsely justified by appeal to privileged premises or experiences from which speculation may take flight. Theological applications of nonfoundational criticism rightly exercise caution toward any agenda of reasoning as organized as a speculative approach with a name, a method, and a content. But the principal issue at stake for such theological criticism is whether and in what ways speculative philosophical programs are compatible or incompatible with a Christian confession's context of meaning. Christian confessions must be wary of any theory whose theological use eclipses the deference appropriately accorded to Christian belief. Frei, Lindbeck, and Thiemann enact this rule by rebuking the customary conduct of theological apologetics in which, they judge, extrabiblical theory usurps narrative authority. By allowing for the possibility of an "ad hoc" approach to apologetics, however, they concede that how a theology *uses* philosophical theories, and not philosophical theory as such, is what might prove detrimental to ecclesial interpretation. If nonfoundational criticism does not invalidate the use of philosophical theories in theology, instructing instead on their *proper* use, then even speculative approaches to theology can be reconciled with its perspective.

Speculative theologies traditionally have been at home in the Catholic tradition, although Protestant theologians increasingly have embraced this approach in the modern period. Speculative theologies typically appeal to philosophical analysis of the human condition as a means of appreciating the contemporary purport of the gospel message. Whether philosophical analysis offers an anthropology (as it does in existentialist reflection), a portrait of historicity (as it does in hermeneutics), or a cosmology (as it does in process thought), its insights are received by the speculative theologian as timely elucidations of the claims of faith expressed in scripture and tradition. Broadly speaking, the speculative approach correlates Christian meaning and philosophical constructions of the human situation to offer a theological interpretation both genuinely Christian and relevant to contemporary experience.

Nonfoundational theologians have been wary of this method, even suggesting that the correlational enterprise itself epitomizes the error of foundationalism. The concern of nonfoundationalists like Frei, Lindbeck, and Thiemann in this regard is not unfounded. Modern apologetics sometimes indulges its secular audience by accommodating Christian explanation to non-Christian expectations. The correlational method is easily employed in ways that accord priority to philosophical construction rather than to the normative canons of Christian interpretation. In such a foundationalist procedure, theology is reduced to philosophical speculation as reasoning outside the Christian context measures that context by its own control beliefs, selecting some Christian beliefs that are compatible with its own and rejecting others that are not. But even if these are real interpretive dangers, there is no reason in principle to think that the practice of correlation need be foundationalist in its results.[14] Speculative theologies could be consistent with the nonfoundational point of view if their appeal to philosophical analysis were ad hoc and governed by the contextuality of Christian meaning. The speculative approach in such an instance would not trust reason to set its agenda but would measure speculative proposals by their conformity to the standard of Christian commitment. Understood thus, speculative theologies need not be judged betrayals of Christian reasoning that take their point of departure from a context other than the Christian. On the contrary, speculative theologies can be read as legitimate descriptions of ecclesial belief, as long as their portrayals of God and world are, in Wolterstorff's terminology, controlled by Christian conviction.

Nonfoundational Inclusivity

If one of the important contributions of nonfoundational criticism to theology is its emphasis on the contextuality of meaning, then theologians need to be aware of how confessional commitments influence judgments about the acceptability of particular approaches to theological method. Classical Reformation theology espouses confessional belief in its suspicion of theological speculation, its doctrine of human sinfulness leading it to reject any capacity in reason for fruitful knowledge of God. In line with this doctrine, Protestant nonfoundationalists are inclined to understand the theological task as exegetical description of the Christian web of belief, itself principally understood as scriptural narrative, and to portray theological speculation as foundationalist in principle. The Catholic tradition's commitment to the doctrinal anthropology of Trent, which understands human nature as fallen and yet responsible to God, affirms reason's capacity to know God with the assistance of grace and so judges theological speculation to be consistent with its background beliefs. One can recognize classical Protestant sensibilities at work in the writings of Frei, Lindbeck, and Thiemann. There is no reason, however, to identify nonfoundational theology with an interpretive approach consistent with the confessional commitments of these theologians, however excellent their work may be. A Roman Catholic nonfoundational theology would share many of the same concerns voiced by Frei, Lindbeck, and Thiemann about the logical integrity of theology. Yet confessional differences would lead its argumentation in different directions. Catholic nonfoundationalists, like their Protestant colleagues, would be committed to theological inference guided by confessional values and on guard against foundationalist justifications of belief. A Catholic nonfoundational theology would offer arguments, interpretations, and conclusions devoted to the particularity by which the Catholic tradition marks its identity.[15] But the Catholic particularity represented in a nonfoundational theology would be more inclined than would the beliefs of classical Protestantism to find speculative insights helpful aids in the expression of its doctrinal contextuality.

Our argument to this point on behalf of nonfoundational inclusivity still may not satisfy those concerned about the exclusivity suggested by a contextual approach to meaning. Nonfoundational theologies may indeed flourish in any confessional setting or admit of a pluralism of methodological approaches. Their perspective on the nature of understanding, though, seems to forbid the universality that many theologians judge to be a value, even a primary value, of their disciplinary claims. From the perspective of this misgiving, the most troublesome aspect of a nonfoundational theology is the exclusivity posed by its most basic epistemological commitments. If the gospel message is affirmed in faith as universally true, then how can a theology representing that message advance only contextual claims? The nonfoundational perspective itself, this question points out, seems inconsistent with a most basic Christian belief and threatens to relativize the truth that Christians profess as their own.

This question and its anticipated answer express the persistent fear that the confessional focus for theology urged by nonfoundationalists leads inescapably to an interpretive exclusivity that limits the claims of Christianity to relative, parochial, and even isolated contexts. This concern, however, confuses the scope of theological claims with their nature. Christians, after all, do make universal claims for the truth of the gospel message. Since the universality of these claims stands as a background belief within the meaningful context of any confession, Christians have an obligation to express this belief in professions of faith, whether they be personal, liturgical, or theological. But the manner in which one commits oneself to that belief, or reasons from it, or gathers evidence for its cogency, or makes judgments about its significance cannot be universal, since these activities are practices tied to particular religious frameworks from which they draw their meaning. Indeed, there is no alternative to these practices except the foundationalist illusion of a universal reasoning to justify belief. The appeal of that illusion readily leads to the error that claims for the universality of Christian truth require an epistemic ground as certain and as universal in its capacity to justify as the scope of the claims themselves. The universal scope of Christian claims would require such a foundation only if these claims needed to be justified in all possible contexts or, to say the same, in a respect that was context-neutral. Only an apologetics motivated by foundationalist assumptions, however, would expect the universal justification of a claim for the universality of Christian truth.

Nonfoundational criticism has shown that beliefs of any sort do not need universal justification in order to be meaningful. A universal or foundationalist justification is a logical impossibility, apparently accomplishable only by bringing the mutual relations in the network of justification to closure by empty assertions for the authority of some mode of noninferential knowledge. Christian claims are, and remain, particular. They, like all claims, are exclusive by their contextuality, in both the meaning they espouse and in the manner of their espousal. Their exclusivity or particularity does not limit the truth of Christian claims to ghettoes of meaning that insiders alone may appreciate and outsiders cannot fathom. The exclusivity of Christian belief does not compromise the universality it claims, ironically as an expression of its very particularity. Christian particularity, though, requires claims for the universality of its truth to be expressions of its belief and not the expectations of a pretentious epistemology. Theologically, this means quite simply that interpretive strategies should not try to be all things to all people, even though the truth these strategies foster proclaims itself as catholic.

The Promise of Nonfoundational Theology

In a recent essay, David Kelsey addresses the issue of exclusivism from a different perspective, as it has been raised by George Lindbeck's critics and, we might add, by the critics of nonfoundational theology in general. Lindbeck's use of the metaphors of "culture" and "language" for the church, his critics point out, "favor theologies of the church that locate its ends within itself."[16] Like all nonfoundational approaches to meaning, Lindbeck's postliberal theology finds ecclesial meaning in a particular culture or language of belief, that is, in the contextuality of Christian commitment it names as its own. To the degree that ecclesial meaning in such a conceptualization is self-referential and even defined over against the pluralism of meanings in the culture at large, Christian values and practices would seem to be captive to their contextuality, unable to recognize their own limitations or need for reform. Lindbeck's intratextual view of meaning seems to assume that Christian practice faithful to that meaning is good. Does the fact of Christian contextuality, however, assure its normativeness? "Does the deep grammar of Christian discourse," the critic asks, "ever become ideologically deformed and itself stand in need of reform?"[17]

These questions, Kelsey believes, misunderstand the metaphorical use to which Lindbeck puts the images of "language" and "culture" in his theology. Lindbeck does not claim that Christianity is a language or a culture, but only that "for purposes of clarifying the problem of Christian identity through change it is illuminating to see ways in which church discourse and church life are *like* a culture or a language."[18] Moreover, Lindbeck's theological proposal assumes that Christian churches are dialogical communities, constantly engaged in a critical conversation among themselves and with their host culture. Yet, Kelsey concedes, as misplaced as the critics' worries about a postliberal theory of doctrine may be, they "are rooted in sound intuition about the limits of the usefulness of the master metaphors funding the [cultural-linguistic] theory."[19] The metaphors of "culture" and "language" primarily enable the conceptualization of Christian particularity as an abiding and yet developing set of beliefs and practices. But their very richness as metaphors permits them to be understood as calls for an ecclesial exclusivism so narrow that, so conceived, the church would be incapable of drawing on the very resources necessary for its self-criticism and reform. These same issues apply as much to nonfoundational theologies in general as they do specifically to Lindbeck's postliberal theology. The call for particularity in a theology "without foundations" intends to remind reflection of its responsibility to its subject matter and to the proper mode of its analysis. *Foundationlessness*, however, might just as well be understood as a technical label for fideism, as an elaborate description of assertions bearing only contempt for free inquiry and the workings of a truly critical reason.

Engaging and Ecumenical

That the meaningfulness of claims and the metaphors by which they are expressed breaks down at certain points should be no surprise to defenders of a nonfoundational understanding of knowledge. The precariousness of metaphors evinces the contextuality of knowledge. The margins of their meaningfulness revealed in varying interpretations are as much markers of contextual specificity as they are boundaries beyond which particular claims lose their intelligibility and begin to evoke criticism. As foundational theologies are inclined toward the error of contentless universalism, nonfoundational theologies may be inclined to the error of exclusivity. One would do better to see the problem of self-criticism, though, as a possible pitfall along the reflective path of a nonfoundational theology rather than as a final judgment on its results. In fact, among the values of a nonfoundational approach to theology one would need to count its appreciation for the diversity of the claims of knowledge engendered by its very insistence on epistemic contextuality.

By highlighting the way knowledge actually does function in limited settings of meaning, a nonfoundational approach to understanding proceeds from an awareness of the complexity of knowledge. Acts of knowing do indeed occur in frameworks of meaning that are limited in a vast number of ways. The commitment that knowing expects as it measures candidates for its assent or rivals to its claims is an expression both of those limitations and, most simply, of its heartfelt loyalty to values, meanings, and practices a community judges to be true. The nonfoundational perspective, however, does not equate the modesty of its functional approach to knowledge with a self-conscious isolationism from contexts different from its own or with a principled resistance to rival claims. In the existential situation in which they find themselves, communities of meaning cannot but face the fact of other meaningful positions and the critical challenges they often present to the community's views. To the degree that these challenges are cogent, communities of meaning modify their previous positions, at times slightly and at times significantly, in order to hold values worthy of belief and action. A nonfoundational understanding of knowledge is, in other words, as dialogically oriented as any hermeneutical theory. It does not assume, however, that intellectual dialogue needs to appeal to universal principles in order to yield understanding, nor does it stand ready to express its own values in the language of others.

Nonfoundational theologies are disposed to recognize that the diversity in doctrinal stands among Christian confessions is an important dimension of any confession's particularity. Identities, whether personal, national, or epistemic, cannot help but be formed negatively as well as positively. Confessional diversity, then, presents not only a host of competing claims to any given confession but also a larger framework of meaning within which confessional claims achieve a sense of their particularity by contrast with the claims of others. Much of the promise of nonfoundational theology lies in its understanding of the complex relations among epistemic claims, or, to express the same idea more loosely, its understanding of just how thick the web of belief is. It is hardly surprising, for example, that the work of George Lindbeck, itself the product of his lifelong involvement in ecumenical dialogue among the churches, has done much to foster appreciation for the theological value of nonfoundationalism. A nonfoundational approach to theological knowledge would be especially partial to ecumenical concerns both for the purpose of fostering mutual understanding among Christian traditions and for the purpose of clarifying the uniqueness of its own commit-ments. Conversation among the confessions brings opportunities to test a confession's particularity and, through the differences that emerge in such a dialogue, to explore the unity in diversity that we call the Christian tradition.[20]

A nonfoundational theology's openness to dialogue need not be limited to the interconfessional realm, where the conversation partners share many of the same presuppositions. If Donald Davidson's reflections on the nature of conceptual schemes are valid, then the particularities of ecclesial meaning cannot be separated in an exclusivist way from the secular meanings of the culture at large, even and perhaps especially those that are hostile in their regard for ecclesial belief. Claims foreign to those espoused by the church, of course, are dialogically related to the church simply by virtue of the fact that the church dwells in a larger society within which discourse inevitably occurs. But from an epistemic perspective informed by Davidson's insights, the claims of the church cannot form a conceptual scheme utterly divorced from others. Even particularistic claims achieve their distinctiveness in relation to a network of belief that extends infinitely in all directions and within which all particular beliefs are mutually related and defined. Within that setting, ecclesial beliefs do indeed possess a specificity that nonfoundational theologies are intent on preserving. Christian background beliefs, though, acquire their meaning in a variety of ways, by confronting, rejecting, sympathizing with, and engaging in ad hoc apologetics toward foreign beliefs. The most cursory reflection on the history of doctrinal development confirms the observation that extraconfessional, as well as interconfessional, dialogue has done much to shape that history and so the very integrity of the Christian tradition. That a nonfoundational theology would be held captive to its own contextuality remains an abiding concern of its interpretive approach. A nonfoundational theology true to its commitments, however, would be ready to engage in dialogue with all parties, no matter how close or distant their sensibilities, as both the practice of its own values and an exercise in understanding.

Christian Faithfulness

As advantageous as a nonfoundational theology may be for promoting substantive ecumenical dialogue and for guiding the proper conduct of apologetics with culture, its promise lies principally in serving as a heuristic for the responsible practice of the theological task. The Enlightenment expected the disciplines to be built on the foundation of a universally intelligible method, itself the formal image of the reason that constructed it. In its logical efforts to reveal the groundlessness of belief, nonfoundational criticism exposes the epistemic vanity of this conception. Modern theology, at least in its typical practice, is the object of this criticism no less than the other disciplines. While most disciplines encounter nonfoundational criticism as the voices of outsiders, theology has come to hear nonfoundational admonishments from voices within its own ranks and expressed in terms of its own concerns. The result, interestingly enough, has been the call for theological practice that is more classical and traditional on the one hand, yet fully in step with the canons of modern criticism on the other. Whether in its premodern or modern executions, theology as a discipline should be more inclined than other modes of knowledge to appreciate and embrace the nonfoundational perspective. Throughout its history, theology has understood itself as faith seeking understanding and so has articulated its contextuality as a dimension of its own disciplinary procedure. Nonfoundationalism encourages theology to be loyal to its age-old reflective strategy, aware of the deficiencies of Cartesian epistemologies, and consistent with its most basic doctrinal beliefs, whether they be ancient or modern in their formulation.

Catholic and Protestant approaches to nonfoundational theology may differ according to their confessional nuances. Each confession can, and indeed should, engage in theological reflection by defending the doctrinal view of foundationlessness it considers authoritative and by criticizing the view of foundations it judges problematic. Both Catholic and Protestant approaches, however, can meet in their appreciation for the critical perspective that the nonfoundational position offers to any theological analysis. The nonfoundational commitment to Christian contextuality at times may be overly cautious about the innovative contributions the theological imagination makes to the development of doctrine and to the changing historicity of the tradition. Its caution, though, is finally an expression of its expectation that the theologian's work be as good as the tradition and responsible to the disciplinary values theology names as its own.[21] Expressed in the imperative mood, this expectation could function as a non-foundational rule for theological practice in any confession or in any analytical style—be it descriptive, speculative, or the thematically critical approaches of political, liberationist, or feminist theologies.

In *The Prescriptions against the Heretics*, Tertullian posed a question that has gained fame as an expression of Christian particularity. "What," he asked, "has Jerusalem to do with Athens?"[22] What, to rephrase a bit, has rational inquiry to do with the church's proclamation of the good news of salvation? For Tertullian this was not an investigative but a rhetorical question. Its obvious answer for Christians, he assumed, was a resounding "Nothing at all!" While some might see Tertullian as an ancient forebear of contemporary nonfoundationalists, I do not think the comparison holds. As understandable as his presumed response may be for a North African Christian living in the age of the martyrs, it does not express the sensibilities of nonfoundationalists but only, perhaps, the fears of their opponents. The promise of nonfoundational theology is that, with Christians like Tertullian, it makes faithfulness to the gospel message a prerequisite of theological inquiry and rejects any effort to satisfy extra-ecclesial expectations of such inquiry that would run contrary to that faithfulness. Unlike Tertullian's stance, the nonfoundational perspective regards culture as a partner in dialogue with Christian reflection, its own understanding of the network of belief cognizant of the myriad relations that join Christian and non-Christian inquiry. In this dialogue, though, in Lindbeck's apt formulation, "It is the text . . . which absorbs the world, rather than the world the text."[23] As Lindbeck reformulates the correlationist enterprise to express his own position, so too might we reformulate Tertullian's famous dictum to express nonfoundational sensibilities. Nonfoundational theologians, on the one hand, expect that Athens will have something to do with Jerusalem, though always on Jerusalem's terms. Jerusalem, on the other hand, will have everything to do with Athens as nonfoundational theologians seek genuinely Christian ways to represent the contextuality of the church's universal claims to the world. Only through a dialogue committed to the particularity of Jerusalem and the fact of Athens can the church aspire to theological reflection worthy of its traditional charge and responsive to the challenge of modern culture.

Notes

1. Nonfoundationalism as Philosophical Criticism

1. Ernest Sosa, "The Raft and the Pyramid: Coherence versus Foundations in the Theory of Knowledge," *Midwest Studies in Philosophy* 5 (1980): 3–25.

2. G. W. F. Hegel, *Hegel's Lectures on the History of Philosophy*, vol. 3, trans. E. S. Haldane and F. H. Simson (New York: Humanities Press, 1968), 220f.

3. René Descartes, *Meditations on First Philosophy*, in *The Philosophical Works of Descartes*, vol. 1, trans. E. S. Haldane and G. R. T. Ross (New York: Dover Publications, 1955), 171f.

4. Descartes, *Discourse on the Method of Rightly Conducting the Reason and Seeking for Truth in the Sciences*, in *The Philosophical Works of Descartes*, 1:106.

5. Ibid., 101.

6. Immanuel Kant, *Groundwork of the Metaphysic of Morals*, trans. H. J. Paton (New York: Harper & Row, 1964), 60.

7. Johann G. Fichte, *Science of Knowledge (Wissenschaftslehre)*, trans. P. Heath and J. Lachs (New York: Appleton-Century-Crofts, 1970), 93.

8. F. W. J. Schelling, *System of Transcendental Idealism (1800)*, trans. P. Heath (Charlottesville: Univ. of Virginia Press, 1978), 211f.

9. G. W. F. Hegel, *Hegel's "Philosophy of Mind" (Part Three of the "Encyclopaedia of the Philosophical Sciences" [1830])*, trans. W. Wallace (Oxford: Clarendon Press, 1971), 178.

10. Charles Sanders Peirce, "A Definition of Pragmatic and Pragmatism," in *Collected Papers of Charles Sanders Peirce*, vol. 5 (Cambridge, Mass.: Harvard Univ. Press, 1978), 3, 6.

11. Peirce, "Lectures on Pragmatism," in *Collected Papers of Charles Sanders Peirce*, 5:13.

12. Peirce, "Some Consequences of Four Incapacities," in *Collected Papers of Charles Sanders Peirce*, 5:156.

13. Ibid.

14. Ibid., 157.

15. Ibid.

16. Ibid., 158. Cf. Peirce, "Questions Concerning Certain Faculties Claimed for Man," in *Collected Papers of Charles Sanders Peirce*, 5:153.

17. Peirce, "How to Make Our Ideas Clear," in *Collected Papers of Charles Sanders Peirce*, 5:253.

18. Ibid., 257.

19. Ibid., 255.

20. William James, *Pragmatism*, in *The Works of William James*, ed. F. Bowers and I. Skrupskelis (Cambridge, Mass.: Harvard Univ. Press, 1975), 97.

21. James, *Essays in Radical Empiricism*, in *The Works of William James*, ed. F. Bowers and I. Skrupskelis (Cambridge, Mass.: Harvard Univ. Press, 1976), 36. Cf. James, *Pragmatism*, 41.

22. John Dewey, *Essays in Experimental Logic* (New York: Dover Publications, 1916), 23.

23. Dewey, *How We Think*, in *John Dewey: The Later Works 1925–1953*, vol. 8, ed. J. Boydston (Carbondale, Ill.: Southern Illinois Univ. Press, 1986), 233.

24. Ludwig Wittgenstein, *Philosophical Investigations*, trans. G. E. M. Anscombe (New York: Macmillan Publishing Co., 1968), 138 (par. 497).

25. Wittgenstein, *On Certainty*, trans. D. Paul and G. E. M. Anscombe (New York: J. & J. Harper, 1969), 30 (par. 225).

26. Wittgenstein, *Philosophical Investigations*, 49 (par. 124), 50 (par. 126).

27. Wilfrid Sellars, "Philosophy and the Scientific Image of Man," in *Science, Perception and Reality* (New York: Humanities Press, 1963), 2.

28. Sellars, "Empiricism and the Philosophy of Mind," in *Science, Perception and Reality*, 140.

29. Ibid.

30. Ibid., 133.

31. Ibid., 148.

32. Ibid., 169.

33. Ibid., 170.

34. Sellars, "The Language of Theories," in *Science, Perception and Reality*, 120.

35. Ibid., 123.

36. Roger F. Gibson, Jr., *The Philosophy of W. V. Quine: An Expository Essay* (Tampa: University Presses of Florida, 1982), 1.

37. W. V. Quine, "Ontological Relativity," in *Ontological Relativity and Other Essays* (New York: Columbia Univ. Press, 1969), 26.

38. Quine, "Things and Their Place in Theories," in *Theories and Things* (Cambridge, Mass.: Harvard Univ. Press, 1981), 2.

39. Quine, "Natural Kinds," in *Ontological Relativity and Other Essays*, 126–27.

40. Quine, "Use and Its Place in Meaning," in *Theories and Things*, 45, 48. Cf. Quine, *Quiddities: An Intermittently Philosophical Dictionary* (Cambridge, Mass.: Harvard Univ. Press, 1987), 130–31: "If the meaning of an expression is to be sought in its use, what is it for two expressions to have the same meaning?

They cannot have exactly the same use, for when we use one we are not using the other. One wants to say rather that they have the same meaning if use of the one in place of the other does not make any relevant difference."
41. Quine, "Ontological Relativity," 27.
42. Quine, "Things and Their Place in Theories," 3.
43. Quine, "Ontological Relativity," 48. The notion of ontological relativity is expressed in Quine's observation that "what makes sense is to say not what the objects of a theory are, absolutely speaking, but how one theory of objects is interpretable or reinterpretable in another" (ibid., 50). Responding in a later writing to ambiguities in his conception of ontological relativity, Quine notes "I can now say what ontological relativity is relative to, more succinctly than I did in the lectures, paper, and book of that title. It is relative to a manual of translation" (Quine, *Pursuit of Truth* [Cambridge, Mass.: Harvard Univ. Press, 1990], 51).
44. Quine, "Things and Their Place in Theories," 22. Cf. Quine, "On Empirically Equivalent Systems of the World," *Erkenntnis* 9 (1975): 327: "There is no extra-theoretic truth, no higher truth than the truth we are claiming or aspiring to as we continue to tinker with our system of the world from within."
45. Quine, "On Empirically Equivalent Systems of the World," 322.
46. Ibid., 313. For a critical discussion of Quine's doctrine of holism, see Hilary Putnam, "Meaning Holism," in *The Philosophy of W. V. Quine*, ed. L. E. Hahn and P. A. Schilpp (La Salle, Ill.: Open Court, 1986), 405–26.
47. Quine, *From a Logical Point of View* (Cambridge, Mass.: Harvard Univ. Press, 1964), 41.
48. Quine, "Epistemology Naturalized," in *Ontological Relativity and Other Essays*, 76.
49. Quine, "Ontological Relativity," 49.
50. Richard Rorty, *Philosophy and the Mirror of Nature* (Princeton, N.J.: Princeton Univ. Press, 1979), 9, 7.
51. Ibid., 157.
52. Ibid., 159.
53. Ibid.
54. Ibid., 293.
55. In the sardonic style with which he often offers critical commentary on the history of philosophy, Rorty notes that "it is fruitless to ask whether the Greek language, or Greek economic conditions, or the idle fancy of some nameless pre-Socratic, is responsible for viewing [authentic] knowledge as *looking* at something (rather than, say, rubbing up against it, or crushing it underfoot, or having sexual intercourse with it)" (ibid., 39).
56. Ibid., 50, 58.
57. Ibid., 132.
58. Ibid., 375.
59. Ibid., 315.
60. Ibid., 356.
61. Ibid., 377.

62. Rorty, *Contingency, Irony, and Solidarity* (New York: Cambridge Univ. Press, 1989), 3–69.

63. Ibid., xv, 100.

64. Rorty, *Philosophy and the Mirror of Nature*, 378; Rorty, *Contingency, Irony, and Solidarity*, 189–98. Cf. Rorty, "Solidarity or Objectivity?" in *Objectivity, Relativism, and Truth: Philosophical Papers*, vol. 1 (New York: Cambridge Univ. Press, 1991), 21–34.

65. Richard J. Bernstein, *Beyond Objectivism and Relativism: Science, Hermeneutics, and Praxis* (Philadelphia: Univ. of Pennsylvania Press, 1983), 8.

66. Ibid., 16–20.

67. William Alston, "Has Foundationalism Been Refuted?" *Philosophical Studies* 29 (1976): 300–302. Cf. Alston, "Two Types of Foundationalism," *Journal of Philosophy* 73 (1976): 171f.

68. Donald Davidson, "On the Very Idea of a Conceptual Scheme (1974)," in *Inquiries into Truth and Interpretation* (Oxford: Clarendon Press, 1984), 184.

69. Ibid., 185.

70. Davidson affirms an inextricable relationship between the human capacities for thought and language: "Languages we will not think of as separable from souls; speaking a language is not a trait a man can lose while retaining the power of thought" (ibid.).

71. Ibid., 195.

72. Ibid., 198.

73. Ibid.

74. Michael Williams, *Groundless Belief: An Essay on the Possibility of Epistemology* (New Haven, Conn.: Yale Univ. Press, 1977), 83–84.

75. Ibid., 89.

76. Ibid., 112.

77. Ibid.

78. Quine, *Pursuit of Truth*, 19.

2.   Nonfoundationalism and Modern Theology

1. In making this judgment, I assume that deconstructive theologians who argue against the authority of scripture cannot be considered Christian theologians. See, for example, Mark C. Taylor, *Erring: A Postmodern A/theology* (Chicago: Univ. of Chicago Press, 1984).

2. Friedrich D. E. Schleiermacher, *On the "Glaubenslehre": Two Letters to Dr. Lücke*, trans. J. Duke and F. Fiorenza (Chico, Calif.: Scholars Press, 1981), 61.

3. See R. Bäumer, "Vermittlungstheologie," in *Lexikon für Theologie und Kirche*, vol. 10, ed. J. Höfer and K. Rahner (Freiburg: Verlag Herder Freiburg, 1965), 719.

4. Monika K. Hellwig, "Foundations for Theology: A Historical Sketch," in *Faithful Witness: Foundations of Theology for Today's Church*, ed. L. O'Donovan and T. Sanks (New York: Crossroad, 1989), 1.

5. Karl Barth, *The Epistle to the Romans*, trans. E. Hoskyns (New York: Oxford Univ. Press, 1972), 9.

6. Ibid., 258.

7. Ibid., 266.

8. Barth, *Church Dogmatics*, I/1, trans. G. Bromiley, 2d ed. (Edinburgh: T. & T. Clark, 1986), 195.

9. Ibid., 214.

10. Ibid., 61–62.

11. Ibid., 34, 251.

12. Ibid., xiii.

13. Barth, *Church Dogmatics*, II/1, trans. T. Parker, *et al.* (Edinburgh: T. & T. Clark, 1985), 5.

14. Barth, *Church Dogmatics*, I/1, 305.

15. Barth, *Church Dogmatics*, II/1, 168.

16. George A. Lindbeck, *The Nature of Doctrine: Religion and Theology in a Postliberal Age* (Philadelphia: Westminster Press, 1984), 16.

17. Ibid., 22.

18. Ibid., 23.

19. Ibid., 18.

20. Ronald F. Thiemann, *Revelation and Theology: The Gospel as Narrated Promise* (Notre Dame, Ind.: Univ. of Notre Dame Press, 1985), 11.

21. Ibid., 10.

22. Ibid., 43.

23. Ibid., 4.

24. Kathryn Tanner, *God and Creation in Christian Theology: Tyranny or Empowerment?* (Oxford: Basil Blackwell, 1988), 126, 120f.

25. Ibid., 47.

26. Ibid., 123.

27. Ibid., 161.

28. Lindbeck, *The Nature of Doctrine*, 118. For an excellent study of this provocative conceptualization of the theological enterprise, see Bruce D. Marshall, "Absorbing the World: Christianity and the Universe of Truths," in *Theology and Dialogue: Essays in Conversation with George Lindbeck*, ed. B. Marshall (Notre Dame, Ind.: Univ. of Notre Dame Press, 1990), 69–102.

29. Lindbeck, *The Nature of Doctrine*, 118.

30. Ibid., 116.

31. Ibid., 115.

32. Ibid., 129.

33. Ibid.

34. Lindbeck, "The Story-Shaped Church: Critical Exegesis and Theological Interpretation," in *Scriptural Authority and Narrative Tradition*, ed. G. Green (Philadelphia: Fortress Press, 1987), 174.

35. Lindbeck, *The Nature of Doctrine*, 130.

36. Ibid., 131.

37. For a discussion of Lindbeck's notion of ad hoc apologetics, see William Werpehowski, "Ad Hoc Apologetics," *The Journal of Religion* 66 (1986): 282–301.

38. Ibid., 115, 132.

39. Thiemann, *Revelation and Theology*, 43–44.

40. Ibid., 44.

41. Ibid.

42. Ibid., 45.

43. Ibid., 43.

44. While Thiemann shares Lindbeck's commitment to a nonfoundational approach to theology, he is unwilling to describe his own work as postliberal. The sensibilities of theological postliberalism, he fears, "engender such skepticism about the possibility of Christian involvement in public life as to render a public theology virtually impossible" (Thiemann, *Constructing a Public Theology: The Church in a Pluralistic Culture* [Louisville: Westminster/John Knox Press, 1991], 24).

45. Thiemann, *Revelation and Theology*, 72.

46. Ibid.

47. Ibid., 75.

48. Hans W. Frei, *The Identity of Jesus Christ: The Hermeneutical Bases of Dogmatic Theology* (Philadelphia: Fortress Press, 1975), 5.

49. Frei, *The Eclipse of Biblical Narrative: A Study in Eighteenth and Nineteenth Century Hermeneutics* (New Haven, Conn.: Yale Univ. Press, 1974), 1.

50. Ibid., 13–14. Frei makes similar arguments on behalf of the centrality of the literal sense of scripture in "The 'Literal Reading' of the Biblical Narrative in the Christian Tradition: Does It Stretch or Will It Break?" in *The Bible and the Narrative Tradition*, ed. F. McConnell (Oxford: Oxford Univ. Press, 1985), 36–77.

51. Frei, *The Eclipse of Biblical Narrative*, 10.

52. Ibid., 103.

53. Frei, *The Identity of Jesus Christ*, 4.

54. Ibid., 20.

55. Ibid., 5.

56. Ibid., 38.

57. Ibid., 124.

58. Ibid., 142.

59. Ibid., 136, 151.

60. Ibid., 102.

61. Stanley Hauerwas, "A Story-Formed Community: Reflections on *Watership Down*," in *A Community of Character: Toward a Constructive Christian Social Ethic* (Notre Dame, Ind.: Univ. of Notre Dame Press, 1981), 9.

62. Ibid., 12.

63. Hauerwas, "Jesus: The Story of the Kingdom," in *A Community of Character*, 50.

64. Ibid., 43.

65. Hauerwas, "The Virtues and Our Communities," in *A Community of Character*, 115. Cf. Hauerwas, "Character, Narrative, and Growth in the Christian Life," in *A Community of Character*, 129–52.

66. Frei, *The Identity of Jesus Christ*, 157, 160.

67. Ibid., 165. Two excellent studies of Frei's theology are George Hunsinger, "Hans Frei as Theologian: The Quest for a Generous Orthodoxy," *Modern Theology* 8 (1992): 103–28; and, in the same volume, Paul Schwartzentruber, "The Modesty of Hermeneutics: The Theological Reserves of Hans Frei," 181– 95.

68. William C. Placher, *Unapologetic Theology: A Christian Voice in a Pluralistic Conversation* (Louisville: Westminster/John Knox Press, 1989), 34.

69. Charles M. Wood, *The Formation of Christian Understanding: An Essay in Theological Hermeneutics* (Philadelphia: Westminster Press, 1981), 51.

3. Nonfoundational Theology in Critical Perspective

1. The fact that Lindbeck, at least, accepts the adjective "postmodern" as an alternate designation for "postliberal" might lead one to conclude that his nonfoundational approach to theology is a rejection of the modern (George A. Lindbeck, *The Nature of Doctrine: Religion and Theology in a Postliberal Age* [Philadelphia: Westminster Press, 1984], 135, n.1). I would argue, though, that nonfoundational theology affirms the most basic traits that modern theologies share and, for that reason, would understand the prefixes in "postliberal" and "nonfoundational" approaches to theology to be expressions of dissatisfaction with, but not rejections of, modern assumptions. Cf. John E. Thiel, *Imagination and Authority: Theological Authorship in the Modern Tradition* (Minneapolis: Fortress Press, 1991), 6–9, 26–30.

2. William P. Alston, "Two Types of Foundationalism," *The Journal of Philosophy* 73 (1976): 166. Emphasis mine.

3. Ibid., 184.

4. Ibid., 183.

5. William P. Alston, "Has Foundationalism Been Refuted?" *Philosophical Studies* 29 (1976): 290f.

6. Ernest Sosa, "The Raft and the Pyramid: Coherence versus Foundations in the Theory of Knowledge," *Midwest Studies in Philosophy* 5 (1980): 14f.

7. Francis Schüssler Fiorenza, *Foundational Theology: Jesus and the Church* (New York: Crossroad, 1986), 285.

8. Cf. Jeffrey Stout, *The Flight from Authority: Religion, Morality, and the Quest for Autonomy* (Notre Dame, Ind.: Univ. of Notre Dame Press, 1981), 33.

9. "I depend on the distinction between what words mean and what they are used to do. I think metaphor belongs exclusively to the domain of use" (Donald Davidson, "What Metaphors Mean," in *Inquiries into Truth and Interpretation* [Oxford: Clarendon Press, 1984], 247).

10. Nicholas Wolterstorff, *Reason within the Bounds of Religion* (Grand Rapids, Mich.: Wm. B. Eerdmanns Pub. Co., 1976), 63.

11. Ibid.

12. Ibid., 66. Cf. Nicholas Wolterstorff, "Can Belief in God Be Rational If It Has No Foundations?" in *Faith and Rationality: Reason and Belief in God*, ed. A. Plantinga and N. Wolterstorff (Notre Dame, Ind.: Univ. of Notre Dame Press, 1983), 155, 170, 176.

13. D. Z. Phillips argues from a philosophical perspective for a fideistic understanding of foundationless belief in which theology is a self-contained enterprise preoccupied exclusively with the concerns of faith. See D. Z. Phillips, *Faith and Philosophical Enquiry* (New York: Schocken Books, 1979); *Faith after Foundationalism* (London and New York: Routledge, 1988). For a critical assessment of Phillips's position, see Hans W. Frei, *Types of Christian Theology*, ed. G. Hunsinger and W. Placher (New Haven, Conn.: Yale Univ. Press, 1992), 46–55.

14. The most cogent argument for this position from a Roman Catholic perspective has been made by Francis Schüssler Fiorenza (*Foundational Theology*, 296f.).

15. Besides F. Fiorenza's work, some examples of Catholic theologies that pursue the nonfoundational approach are Frans Josef van Beeck, S.J., *God Encountered: A Contemporary Catholic Systematic Theology*, vol. 1: *Understanding the Christian Faith* (San Francisco: Harper & Row, 1989); Nicholas Lash, *Easter in Ordinary: Reflections on Human Experience and the Knowledge of God* (Notre Dame, Ind.: Univ. of Notre Dame Press, 1990); James J. Buckley, *Seeking the Humanity of God: Practices, Doctrines, and Catholic Theology* (Collegeville, Minn.: Liturgical Press, 1992). Van Beeck makes Catholic liturgy the center of theological reflection and understands cultic practice to be the matrix of Christian witness in conduct and creed. Lash puts the philosophical reflections of William James, Newman, von Hügel, and Buber among others to practical use to elucidate the sacramental character of human experience, specifically informed by the normative Christian experience of God. Buckley, who of the three develops his views with explicit appeal to the nonfoundational perspective, argues that theological inquiry must be a practice of Catholic particularity that, in faithful commitment to the teachings of tradition, seeks God universally within the many contexts in which life is lived.

16. David H. Kelsey, "Church Discourse and Public Realm," in *Theology and Dialogue: Essays in Conversation with George Lindbeck*, ed. B. Marshall (Notre Dame, Ind.: Univ. of Notre Dame Press, 1990), 26.

17. Ibid., 27.

18. Ibid. Emphasis mine.

19. Ibid., 29.

20. An interesting essay on the ecumenical use of Lindbeck's theology is Michael Root, "Identity and Difference: The Ecumenical Problem," in *Theology and Dialogue*, 165–90.

21. Thiel, *Imagination and Authority*, 162.

22. Tertullian, *The Prescriptions against the Heretics*, in *Early Latin Theology*, Library of Christian Classics, vol. 5, ed. S. Greenslade (Philadelphia: Westminster Press, 1956), 36.

23. Lindbeck, *The Nature of Doctrine*, 118.

Glossary

Apologetics—the theological task of explaining Christian beliefs to those outside the church; since the Enlightenment often by finding a common ground in general human experience as the basis of explanation

A posteriori—derived from sense experience, especially knowledge so derived

A priori—independent of sense experience; in this discussion, innate ideas, structures of the mind, and the knowledge derived from them

Cartesian—of or pertaining to the philosophy of Rene Descartes; in this discussion, especially that philosophy's assumption that knowledge must be based on indubitable first principles

Empiricism—a philosophy that makes sense experience the source and criterion of knowledge

Epistemic—of or pertaining to knowledge, especially the constitution, conditions, or construction of knowledge

Epistemology—a theory or explanation of the nature of knowledge and how we know

Foundations—in epistemology, beliefs or experiences that are certain in themselves, and that in turn support the beliefs derived from them in an extended system of knowledge

Hermeneutics—the theory or practice of interpretation, especially the interpretation of linguistic forms of expression

Idealism—a philosophy that makes ideas or mental data the source and criterion of knowledge

Intratextual—a theological value that makes scripture and doctrine normative, while resisting comparable claims of normativity for general human experience

Justification—the philosophical task of providing grounds for the assumptions, procedures, and conclusions of reasoning

Metaphysics—a speculative theory about the nature of reality

Noetic—of or pertaining to the mind, especially the mind's ideas

Noninferential—a description of beliefs that are not the conclusion of step-by-step reasoning but whose truth is directly or immediately evident

Truth-claims—beliefs that purport to describe the way things are

Select Bibliography

1. Nonfoundationalism as Philosophical Criticism

For a brief overview of the issues at stake in the "foundations of knowledge" debate, see William C. Placher, *Unapologetic Theology: A Christian Voice in a Pluralistic Conversation* (Louisville: Westminster/John Knox Press, 1989), 24–38. C. F. Delaney, *et al.*, *The Synoptic Vision: Essays on the Philosophy of Wilfrid Sellars* (Notre Dame, Ind.: Univ. of Notre Dame Press, 1977), discusses Sellars's philosophy from several points of view. A select bibliography of the works of Willard Van Orman Quine can be found in *The Philosophy of W. V. Quine*, ed. L. E. Hahn and P. A. Schilpp (La Salle, Ill.: Open Court, 1986), 669–86. In addition to Rorty's groundbreaking *Philosophy and the Mirror of Nature* (1979) and *Contingency, Irony, and Solidarity* (1989), readers will want to consult his *Consequences of Pragmatism (Essays 1972–1980)* (Minneapolis: Univ. of Minnesota Press, 1982) and two more recent collections of papers: *Objectivity, Relativism, and Truth: Philosophical Papers*, vol. 1; and *Essays on Heidegger and Others: Philosophical Papers*, vol. 2 (Cambridge: Cambridge Univ. Press, 1991). For a discussion of Donald Davidson's work, see *Truth and Interpretation: Perspectives on the Philosophy of Donald Davidson*, ed. E. LePore (Oxford: Basil Blackwell, 1986).

2. Nonfoundationalism and Modern Theology

James J. Buckley, "Revisionists and Liberals," in *The Modern Theologians: An Introduction to Christian Theology in the Twentieth Century*, vol. 2, ed. D. Ford (Oxford: Basil Blackwell, 1989), 89–102, discusses the sensibilities of typically modern approaches to the theological task. For an overview of some of the nonfoundational theologians treated in this chapter, see William C. Placher, "Postliberal Theology," in *The Modern Theologians*, 115–28. A select bibliography of the works of Hans Frei can be found in *Scriptural Authority and Narrative Interpretation*, ed. G. Green (Philadelphia: Fortress Press, 1987), 199–201. In addition to this *Festschrift*, there is a collection of articles and responses devoted to Frei's thought in *Modern Theology* 8 (1992): 103–214. A select bibliography of the works of George Lindbeck can be found in *Theology and Dialogue: Essays in Conversation with George Lindbeck*, ed. B. Marshall (Notre Dame, Ind.: Univ. of Notre Dame Press, 1990), 283–98. There are two symposia of articles on Lindbeck's *The Nature of Doctrine* (1984) in *The Thomist* 49 (1985): 392–472, and *Modern Theology* 4 (1988): 107–209.

3. Nonfoundational Theology in Critical Perspective

For critical evaluations of nonfoundational theology, see James M. Gustafson, "The Sectarian Temptation: Reflections on Theology, the Church, and the University," *Proceedings of the Catholic Theological Society of America* 40, ed. G. Kilcourse (1985): 83–94; B. A. Gerrish, "Review Article: *The Nature of Doctrine*," *The Journal of Religion* 68 (1988): 87–92; Mark I. Wallace, *The Second Naiveté: Barth, Ricoeur, and the New Yale Theology* (Macon, Ga.: Mercer Univ. Press, 1990); Gary Comstock, "Truth or Meaning: Ricoeur versus Frei on Biblical Narrative," *The Journal of Religion* 66 (1986): 117–40. Bruce Marshall, *Christology in Conflict: The Identity of a Saviour in Rahner and Barth* (Oxford: Basil Blackwell, 1987), offers a helpful analysis of the issue of universality and particularity in theological claims.

Index